Once Upon a Farm

Once Upon a Farm

LESSONS ON GROWING LOVE, LIFE, AND HOPE ON A NEW FRONTIER

RORY FEEK

W PUBLISHING GROUP

AN IMPRINT OF THOMAS NELSON

Published in Nashville, Tennessee, by W Publishing Group, an imprint of Thomas Nelson.

Thomas Nelson titles may be purchased in bulk for educational, business, fund-raising, or sales promotional use. For information, please e-mail SpecialMarkets@ThomasNelson.com.

The Bible verse quoted in "Climbing Trees" is Matthew 19:26, King James Version. Public Domain.

Any Internet addresses, phone numbers, or company or product information printed in this book are offered as a resource and are not intended in any way to be or to imply an endorsement by Thomas Nelson, nor does Thomas Nelson vouch for the existence, content, or services of these sites, phone numbers, companies, or products beyond the life of this book.

ISBN 978-0-7852-2109-8 (TP)
ISBN 978-0-7852-1674-2 (eBook)

Library of Congress Cataloging-in-Publication Data

Names: Feek, Rory Lee, author.
Title: Once upon a farm : lessons on growing love, life, and hope on a new
    frontier / Rory Feek.
Description: Nashville, Tennessee : W Publishing Group, [2018]
Identifiers: LCCN 2018000691 | ISBN 9780785216728 (hardcover)
Subjects: LCSH: Feek, Rory Lee. | Singers—United States—Biography. | Country
    musicians—United States—Biography.
Classification: LCC ML420.F315 A3 2018 | DDC 782.421642092 [B] —dc23 LC record
    available at https://lccn.loc.gov/2018000691

Printed in the United States of America

19 20 21 22 23 LSC 5 4 3 2 1

For our three beautiful daughters: Heidi, Hopie, and Indiana.
Even when you have babies, you will still be my babies.

For the blonde and the brown and the pigtails that rise
For the blue and the green and almond-shaped eyes
For the future and the past and the moments you're in
From your father, your daddy, your Papa and friend.

For the pain and the sorrow and the empty you feel
For the joy and the happy and the magic that's real
For the love and the hope that never will end
From your father, your daddy, your Papa and friend.

For the daughter and mother, the lover and wife
For the questions, the answers, and the riddles of life
For the grownup and the child that lives deep within
From your father, your daddy, your Papa and friend.

Contents

Foreword   ix

Coming Home   1
Day One   5
A Bigger Love   11
One Plus One   17
My College Years   21
Semper Fi   25
Barber Shopping   31
Choo-Choo Training   37
Dollars and Sense   41
Unwritten   45
Dearly Beloved   51
Fixer-Upper   53
Location, Location, Location   59
Three Chords and the Truth   61
I Hold the Pen   65
Video Rewind   69
Daddy, What If?   73
Monday, Monday   77
Brilliant Limitations   81
The *Bus* Stops Here   85
Mayberry   89
Some Barn   95
Heart Break   99
Farmhouse Christmas   103
Bib & Buckle   107

CONTENTS

Presidential Treatment   113

I Love You, I Love You, I Love You   115

Modern Family   119

Our Very Own   123

Heartlight   127

Bare-Metal Truth   131

Brand-New Bus   135

Speak Love   143

Miss Congeniality   147

Hymn and Her   149

Uncle Dale   153

Boy in the Mirror   157

Climbing Trees   161

My Worst Nightmare   165

Happy Mother's Day, Dad   169

Boots and Bibles   173

Fire Kids   177

Teaching Me How to Love You   183

Love Does   187

Gentleman Farmer   191

Field of Dreams   195

Special Eyes   199

Home School   203

Unfamous   207

WWJD?   211

Once Upon a Farm   215

Lifesteading   217

Sign of the Cross   221

From the Cradle to the Grave   225

Always and Forever   227

Last Letters   231

About the Author   235

Foreword

I've noticed that most books begin with an
opening section called the foreword. Which is
perfect for this book, too, because forward is
where we must go even when we don't want to.

They say you shouldn't judge a book by its cover, but for this book, I disagree. What's on the front of the book you're holding pretty much sums up what's on the pages inside, not because the little girl on my shoulders is adorable and the farmhouse and barns behind it are so picturesque. But because the story of that picture is kinda like the story that is shared in the book. It was a roller-coaster ride with enthusiastic high fives and disappointing loss, the testing of our faith and the realization that everything would be okay, even when it wasn't . . . just like the fifteen-year-plus story that has unfolded at our farm since we bought it in 1999. But for the photo, all those things happened in less than twelve hours.

It was just before sunset about six months ago, and we were in the back field. Me and Indy, the publisher's art director, a few friends, and our photographer buddy, Bryan Allen. BA, as his friends call him, is a world-class cameraman. Whether it's still photography of someone's wedding day or a major sporting event being shot on video, BA will capture what you're looking for and then some.

Since it was May, and the days were getting longer, and hotter, I told BA he might have a window of a half hour or so of really good light in the back field as the sun's setting, but, unfortunately, our three-year-old daughter Indiana's window is probably gonna be much shorter. A few minutes, max. Maybe only a few seconds. And that's exactly what happened. Around 7:30 p.m., we found a spot in the tall grass just over the shoulder of the fenced-in cemetery, and I picked her up on my shoulders as someone told Indy to smile. As the camera aperture clicked, Indy smiled great big for a moment or two—then proceeded to fall apart.

Out of the corner of her eye, she had seen the small wooden swing hanging from a tree in the cemetery where her mama is buried and was ready to head there and swing like we did most evenings. "Swing," she said, and tears started streaming down her face. I pulled her down into my arms and tried to console her, but she wasn't having it. The shoot was over. At least for her it was.

As I held her, BA scrolled through the dozen or so pics he'd snapped in those few seconds with his camera. "Check this out!" he said, as he held the back of his Canon 5D up so Kristen from HarperCollins and the others could see. And then he walked over and showed it to me also. Somehow, he'd managed to get the absolute perfect picture in only a matter of seconds.

"Beautiful, BA," I said. "I'm gonna take her to swing for a while. Maybe we could try taking a few more shots there."

And so I pushed her on the little green swing for twenty minutes or so and then put her in her wagon and started back toward the house. BA kept shooting through it all, and Indy didn't seem to mind. But I could tell, the "magic" had probably already happened, and though he was taking hundreds, maybe thousands more pics, we already had the one that was gonna be the cover of the book.

About halfway back to the house, I sat down by Indiana in the wagon, and we talked and played for a few minutes in the high grass as

BA changed batteries and cards in his camera. He took a few more pics, and then we finished our walk home and were soon in the kitchen with Indy in her high chair eating grapes, and I was doing some dishes that had piled up in the sink from the dinner we all had enjoyed together before walking out into the field to do the photo shoot.

By then the sun was down behind the trees, and it was nearly dark. I could see a few of the guys still standing in the field, walking around where we had last shot—looking for something. My cousin, and our manager, Aaron, came through the back door with a strange look on his face.

"What's wrong?" I said.

"Well . . . ," he answered. "It seems that when we changed cards out in the field, the first card dropped in the grass, and we can't find it."

I looked out the window again. Realizing that the grass hadn't been mowed in weeks and it wouldn't be long before it would be cut for hay.

"Is that the one with the . . ." I started to ask.

"Yep," Aaron answered.

Indiana was watching the whole conversation and loving it, I think.

"More," she said as she held her little plastic bowl up for me to refill with grapes.

An hour later Indy was in her crib asleep, and I had joined the rest of the guys in the field with flashlights and iPhone lights, looking for a one-inch-by-one-inch piece of black plastic in fifty acres of foot-and-a-half tall grass. *This is impossible*, I thought. *Like finding a needle in a thousand haystacks.*

"We're never gonna find this, are we?" I asked no one in particular.

"Nope," BA answered.

"Okay, so what's our plan B?" I said, knowing that we hadn't really thought to make one.

"Well . . . ," he answered, "we can look through all the other pics I took and see if there's one that we like as much or better . . ." He was shaking his head. "I already know the answer to that."

"Or . . . ," he continued, "I guess we can set up another day to get together and shoot some more." I knew that would be tough to do anytime soon since Bryan lives in Knoxville and HarperCollins had a deadline for the cover. I had a few more months to work on the writing of the book—what it was gonna say. But what it was gonna look like—they needed for a big sales meeting in just a few days.

We stayed out there in the pitch black, looking for another half hour or so, then headed in to the house. Ready to call it a night. "We can look again in the morning," I said, knowing it was hopeless.

Aaron, BA, and I, along with my wife's best friend, Julie, stayed up for a long time talking and laughing in the living room about how ridiculous it was that we had lost the card. We'd shot countless album covers and hundreds of hours of TV shows and films together . . . not to mention what each of us had done on our own . . . and never lost an SD card before—let alone in the middle of a hayfield as the sun went down.

It would've been heartbreaking if it wasn't so comical. We all knew that in the grand scheme of things—compared to what my family had been through in the past year or so—this was nothing. But it was an interesting dilemma, if nothing else.

As the sun came up the next morning, BA stumbled into the kitchen and casually looked out the window over the sink. "Oh no!" he said as he threw on his shoes and flew out the back door. I peeked out the window to see our horses, Moon and Ria, standing in the exact spot where we had been looking. The place where we'd changed cards or, at least, where we thought it had happened. He was soon standing right beside them, trying to shoo away a couple of thousand-pound animals from "the scene of the crime."

I started laughing as I watched. Pretty soon Aaron and Julie and Daniel were in the field joining him—walking in circles—as I started breakfast for the baby and myself.

Twenty minutes later Indiana was again beside me in her high chair, finishing her oatmeal as I ate mine.

"You're not gonna believe this," I heard BA say, as he walked in the back door followed by Aaron and Julie and Daniel—all with big smiles on their faces.

"You gotta be kidding me!" I said.

"Nope." And in his hand was the culprit. A black 64-gigabyte SanDisk card with the magic picture inside.

"How about that," I said, as I turned to look at Indy. She just smiled and held up her bowl. "More, Papa."

●

Ain't that how life is? It's never really easy. It takes twists and turns and goes in directions you don't want it to go in. You're hoping for smooth sailing today, and the wind suddenly kicks up and spins your boat around in a completely different direction. And all you can do is hang on and try not to capsize.

It used to disappoint me, that life couldn't be simpler. But I've learned to embrace it. To do more than embrace it. To love that life is that way. That the crazy ride is what life actually is, when it is at its best.

We could've walked into the back field and took pics for an hour, then gone inside and looked through what we'd shot and picked our favorite for the cover and e-mailed it to the publisher. That would've been easy. But it wouldn't have been much of a story. Not a great story anyway.

Stories are always better when they are filled with conflict and your character is tested. When your character's character is tested. Looking back at all the movies I love or stories I've heard that moved me . . . none of them are simple journeys where someone wants something and then gets what they wanted. They are stories filled with drama and heartbreak. With joy and suffering and lots and lots of time spent overcoming obstacles. Someone wants something but can't seem to get it. And so they go in a different direction. And that leads to something they didn't expect. They think they are lost. And they are. Until they realize that the wrong path has led them to the place they were trying to get to in the first place. And on and on. It isn't simple, but it's gripping, with a hint of the kind of mystery in a Stephen King story and the magical romance of a Nicholas Sparks novel, all rolled into one.

Like the story of the photo on the cover of this book, our story is not simple. My story. And my wife's and my family's. It is complicated. Very complicated. I spent 240 pages telling a lot of it in my first book, *This Life I Live*. And I loved telling it, but there's more. So, so much more.

The story of the writing of this book has also been much more complicated than I thought it'd be. And a lot harder. I had thought I knew what it was going to be about, and then, all of a sudden, I realized that I didn't. It was like the picture I had in my mind had gotten lost in a hayfield and I was stuck with no plan B. Not sure what I was going to do. But I kept looking. Staying up late at night with the lamp beside my desk on, typing on my laptop, searching in the weeds of doubt that can fill our minds at times for what it was supposed to be . . . supposed to say. And just when I was about to lose hope and give up . . . there it was. And here it is.

It turns out that the answer was actually right in front of me all along.

The beginning is the end.

To tell the story of how we are moving forward and of the hope that is unfolding now, I have to go backward and start with the end of another great story of hope. Because this one couldn't be told if that one didn't happen. One cannot be without the other. We couldn't have this life we're learning to live on our own if we didn't have the life we lived with my wife, Joey, before it.

And so I will begin with where our story starts . . . at the end of another story.

Coming Home

Home is where the heart wants to be.

From my wife's hometown of Alexandria, Indiana, to our farmhouse in Tennessee is 388 miles. About a six-hour drive if you don't find yourself stopped for construction or the half dozen or so Starbucks signs that call out your name along the way. All interstate, except the first couple of miles; it's not a bad drive really. I've always kinda enjoyed it. The endless Indiana corn and soybean fields on both sides of the blacktop, the big iron bridge that crosses the river into Louisville and, ultimately, drops into the Cumberland Plateau, and seeing the lit-up cityscape of Nashville. Home. Or, at least, we knew home was not far away.

My first time to make the drive was in the spring of 2002, when my two teenage daughters climbed into my Ford Expedition with me and the girl I was dating named Joey; we headed north to meet her parents and sisters and see the home and community where she grew up. And now . . . here it was early March 2016, a lifetime later . . . and we were driving back. This time without Joey.

The morning had started like most of the mornings had over the past few months. I felt the soft vibration of the alarm I'd set on my iPhone that was lying on the bed beside me and saw the amber numbers 4:45 a.m. blinking at me. I slipped out of bed and quietly opened the door so as not to wake the baby who was sleeping in a Pack 'n Play a few feet away. Rubbing my eyes, I headed for the kitchen and started some water boiling to make a French press. While the water heated up, I made my way across the living room and into the big room on the other side of the house. As I rounded the corner, I could hear the beeping sound of the IV that had been attached to my wife for nearly four months now. And I could see her in the moonlight.

Her hospital bed was positioned next to a large picture window with a view of the Gaithers' pond, and the reflection of a half-moon silhouetted my beautiful bride as she slept. Her oldest sister, Jody, a registered nurse on a leave of absence, was in the large bed across the room sleeping, too, if you can call it that. Always rising and jumping up to take care of her little sister at the slightest unusual sound. I stood in the doorway and just listened for a long time, thinking to myself, *How much more, Lord, does Joey have to go through?*

By 1 p.m., God had answered that question. Her breathing became irregular and a rattling sound in her chest filled the room. "It's happening," Jody said. And I found myself kneeling by my wife's bedside talking to her as her breathing became slower and slower. Some of Joey's family were there. Jody, her father, Jack, and younger sister Jessie—the ones who could drop what they were doing and get there fast enough—along with our bus driver, Russell, and our oldest daughter, Heidi, who had arrived the night before and was thankful, though a bit nervous, to be here when her mother was passing from this world into the next.

"It's okay, honey, just let go . . . ," I whispered as my fingers softly stroked the place where her once-beautiful hair had been. "We'll be okay, everything's gonna be okay." And moments later, the rattle stopped and along with it the life of the greatest person I've ever known.

What happened next was a bit of a blur. Nothing. Everything. We all held hands and said a prayer for the gift that she had been. For the gift that she would always be. Someone called the family pastor, Jerry Young, and Mike Owens from the funeral home across town. One arrived wearing an Indiana basketball jersey with hugs and prayers and the other in a dark suit with a kind smile and a stretcher that waited outside. Mike gently reminding us, "There's no rush . . . take as much time as you need." And we did.

The snow was falling a few hours later as our Chevy Suburban merged onto I-65, headed south out of Indianapolis. Heidi was riding shotgun and Indiana was in the car seat directly behind her. The baby silently watching *Finding Nemo* on the video screen that folds down from above. Her eyes barely open—not because she was sleepy but because a crust had slowly been taking over her eyelids since we climbed in the truck a few hours before. Pinkeye.

The sign said twenty-seven miles to Bowling Green. I'd called Theron Hutton, our family doctor back in Tennessee, to ask him what to do. "Wipe them clean, and I'll call in a prescription you can pick up at the next big town," he'd said. And so I kept an eye on the road in front of me and one on the little face in the rearview mirror.

She looked pitiful. Beautiful and precious, but pitiful. One eye already swollen shut and the other nearly there. There was no sign of any unusual pinkness in her little almond eyes when we hugged Joey's mama and sister Jody goodbye a few hours earlier and pulled out the driveway of the brick house that our family had been living, and dying, in for months. The gunk in and around her eyes had slowly grown thicker over the miles, just like the heaviness of what had just happened and where we were going had been growing in our hearts and minds as we drove.

"You doin' alright, Dad?" Heidi asked as she smiled softly and put her hand in mine.

Strength wasn't one of our oldest daughter's strong points, but today she had been incredibly brave and strong. She had surprised even herself, I think.

"I'm okay," I answered. And I was. And I wasn't.

Just three weeks ago we had been blowing out the candles on Indy's second birthday cake . . . and my beautiful wife, Joey, had been there to see it happen. She was just a shell of herself by then, but she was there. We all could see the joy in her eyes as two dozen family members gathered around and sang "Happy Birthday" to a pair of little almond eyes that only knew sign language.

It had been a long goodbye, and I was thankful for it. It could have been fast. Painless for her. But the pain for us would've been greater, I think.

And so we drove on in silence. With peace in our hearts.

Day One

A walk to remember . . .

MARCH 5, 2016.

We pulled into our driveway at about two in the morning. The moon was shining brightly in the sky, illuminating our big white farmhouse and the red barns that surround it. It looked like a scene out of a movie. A movie that I knew well. The setting of an incredible love story that I never would've dreamed I'd get to be part of when we first bought the place in 1999.

I arose at sunrise just a few hours later and loaded the K-Cup coffee machine and hit start. As I waited for my Marcy Jo's mug to fill, I glanced out the kitchen window onto the back deck. Everything was the same. Almost just like we had left it five months earlier. The round metal table and chair set where Joey spent many spring mornings filling eggshells with soil and tiny vegetable seeds, preparing for the garden that she loved so. And the red Crosley glider beside the west wall of the farmhouse, covered in peeling paint, where we had held the baby in our arms countless mornings and thanked God for her and the beautiful life He had given to us.

With my coffee in hand, I slipped on a pair of rubber boots that were sitting by the door and took a stroll down the steps and into the yard. The woodshed beside our Hardy Heater was still filled with the cords of hardwood we had cut the summer before but never used, and the henhouse that was once filled with as many as a hundred small brooder chicks lay empty. The few hens that had remained last fall, we'd given away to neighbors, knowing that we wouldn't be home to take care of them.

I cracked opened the door of Joey's garden shed: her domain for a dozen springs and summers. The place where a good portion of the food in our bellies and freezer had originated. Her hand tools and baskets and canning supplies were all there, but covered in dust. Many of them untouched for the past two years or so.

Nearby was the fire pit where we'd grilled expensive rib eyes and sipped cheap wine and the clothesline where men's overalls, women's jeans, and cloth diapers had once flapped in the soft breeze. On the side of a cedar tree was a bird feeder made from a Wyoming license plate that Joey and I had bought at a fair we played out west and below that a large pig made entirely of horseshoes—a thousand-pound piece of art from a fan who was an artist from Florida. He had brought it to us as a gift and backed his trailer into the yard and set it there, never to be moved again.

I walked through the gate into the garden. Recently mowed by Thomas, our trusty farmhand who'd been with us for more than five years, it looked more like a grassy field than the huge rectangle of measured rows, filled with corn and cukes and beets and beans, that it usually was. Four rusting T-posts marked where the corners had been as did a row of tall grass with a hand-printed sign that read "ASPARAGUS" that Joey had put up years before to keep me or anyone else from mowing down the precious plants that grew back year after year.

Behind the garden were the fruit trees and blackberry bushes we had planted. And the wooden raised-bed boxes that I had built for Joey to grow strawberries. And from where I stood, I could see three of my wife's favorite birthday gifts from years past. Memories of her sweet smile lighting up the farm.

The first one, a ten-by-twelve-foot greenhouse I had found a picture of online and built for her three years ago. I had no idea what I was doing, but I made countless trips to Home Depot and spent days cutting and recutting joists because it was something she had always wanted. Needed, actually. I gave it to her for her birthday in early September 2013. By the time we turned the page of the calendar that hangs on our back door to October, there was spinach and kale growing inside. She really got to use it only one full summer, but she loved it and knew that it could take her favorite season of the year—garden season—and extend it a bit on both ends, and that excited her.

The second birthday gift—a hundred-year-old outhouse with a hand-painted sign that said "Potting House"—still sat at the top of the rise by the windmill. I'd found it in a wooded lot in Nolensville in late August 2005. It was covered in vines, and you wouldn't have even known it was there unless someone told you. The man who owned the property said he'd give it to me if I could find a way to haul it away. I had a truck and a trailer and knew it wasn't just trash; it was a part of someone's family. Someone's story. And rather than letting it get set on fire or carried to the dump, I knew it needed to be part of someone else's story. Someone who would appreciate it. And I knew just the person.

There's a series of pictures in a photo album somewhere, and an even clearer one in my mind, of me with my hands over Joey's eyes on her thirtieth birthday. Me saying, "Are you ready?" then pulling my hands down and saying, "Happy birthday, honey!" and her throwing her arms around my neck. Still on the trailer from pulling it out of the woods with my neighbor Spencer's help, Joey loved it and knew exactly where to put it and what to put inside. And now all the years later, I didn't have to walk across the yard to know that it, too, was still filled with canning jars and tobacco sticks and twine along with other things she had a thousand uses for around the farm.

The last of the three isn't just one birthday gift; it's two. Just north of the garden stands a large barn made mostly of recycled wood from a dismantled hundred-year-old tobacco barn that had stood on the property.

Once filled with lawn mowers, garden tillers, and a wood splitter, the new, old barn now houses two quarter horses named Moon and Ria. Originally from Texas, the mares were owned by close friends of ours who gifted them to me last fall so I could gift them to Joey. We were in Newnan, Georgia, at the time. Joey was deep in the middle of six weeks of chemo and radiation following a ten-hour surgery that she had undergone in Chicago two months earlier, and her fortieth birthday was only a few weeks away. She loved horses and had one named Velvet when she was a teenage girl and had always wanted another, but it had just never come to be. We were always too busy and she was much too practical to worry about making that dream come true up until then. But time was precious now and I knew that there was a good chance it was going to be "now or never." And so I drew up some plans to open a wall of that barn and put in two horse stalls and a small paddock surrounding them. At a Cracker Barrel one morning, I scribbled out where the stalls could go and texted a picture of it to Thomas. And then I made a call to our friends Ray and Linda in Texas. By the time we came home on Joey's birthday weekend two weeks later, it was a horse barn, and soon after, a red and a blue roan were eating hay inside two beautiful stalls that Thomas had built.

Joey had got to ride them only one time. She and I both saddled up and rode into the field that day beside each other, her on the red and me on the blue, holding hands, riding off into the sun that was setting just behind the cemetery that we rode out to, circled, and rode back. A trip that now seems to have foreshadowed the ride our lives were about to take.

From the garden I could see the horses were still there. A bit chunkier than they were last fall since the fields were lush with grass and there'd been no one to ride them, but they looked healthy and happy as can be in their new home. I walked over, and they came to me. Moon put her muzzle into my armpit, and I rubbed behind her ear. "Good to see you, girl," I said, as she whinnied softly—my eyes focused on the round wooden fence with the headstones inside of it just across the gate and through the field.

I walked through the paddock and opened the large gate to let the horses out. They sized me up at first, as they passed through the gate, then started moving a bit faster until they both took off running, and I watched them. Not just running but flying. Just thankful to be free. To be alive.

They stopped and settled in a spot in the center of the back field, and I set my coffee cup on a wooden post and started for the cemetery. When we bought the farmhouse in the fall of 1999, I had originally put a small fence around the nine headstones that were there. Built to keep cows from getting in and pushing the stones down. I had recently had that fence torn down and a new, larger one put up. It was the call I made to John Osborne, our local fence builder, from the hallway of Ball Memorial Hospital in Muncie about four months before. The news we had just received was more of the bad kind, and after another surgery we'd be bringing Joey back home, along with hospice, to her mama's house. At the time the doctors thought Joey would be here for only a few more weeks, max. So I told John, "I know you're busy, but hurry, if you can."

He was at our house the next day, and within a few days after that, the large three-rail fence that I was now looking at for the first time had been installed. "Make it a good bit bigger, John," I had told him. "Room for her . . . and for me one day . . . and maybe our children and theirs."

Not a phone call I wanted to make but one that I was thankful I did. The fence was beautiful, and there was a wonderful shady area in the front where we would soon add one more stone and name to the others that marked those buried there.

The sun was still barely rising as I opened the gate and walked in and looked around. There in the center of a small grove of sassafras trees were the headstones of Calvin and Sarah Hardison, who originally built and lived in our farmhouse, and their daughter, Ida, and her husband, William, and a few others. Names associated with this farm for much of the 1800s and barely into the next century. The earliest date on the Hardisons' stones was for their four-year-old son, Orlando Boon, buried in 1862, and the last one was Sarah's, dated 1906. And in front of those was one made of much newer marble with my mother Rita's name on it from where we had buried some of her ashes in 2014.

I found a spot on a makeshift bench we had put out there years earlier and sat down. Not really believing that this was happening.

But it was.

Joey had passed away the day before, on a Friday . . . and that coming Tuesday afternoon we would lay her to rest here. It was surreal. All of it was. I kept thinking of the dozens of times through the years that Joey and I had walked out to the cemetery and talked about being buried beside each other in this spot someday. Dreaming about someday. A day that seemed hard to even imagine. But now here we were.

And I couldn't help but think about another time that I had sat in almost this exact spot as part of a music video for "When I'm Gone," a song we had recorded that imagined a day when the singer had passed away and the man in the story was left alone. We had filmed the music video at our farmhouse. In our bedroom . . . on the porch overlooking the back field. And I had made pretty much the same walk I made this morning and ended up at the same cemetery, sitting in almost exactly the same spot. Acting. Imagining for the camera, and the sake of the song—a life without my beautiful wife. A pretty day very much like today. Except now I wasn't imagining it. The whole song had come to be, almost word for word.

I talk often, to pretty much anyone who will listen, about the magic of songwriting and of storytelling. Of not knowing where the story's going and how, if you have faith, the story will write itself better than you can write it. And how life is the same way. If you let it be.

At least my life has been. Joey's and mine together has.

I sat there for a long time thinking about the days ahead of us. And the years behind us. All that has happened. And all that is going to happen that I don't know anything about. And all the lessons I've learned. The ones I'm still learning.

And how now, a new story was about to unfold. As one chapter was closing, a new one was beginning, and like it or not, my only option was to turn the page and read on.

A Bigger Love

Love is bigger than fear.

It was a day or two after we buried Joey. And I was sitting at the kitchen table with our middle daughter Hopie. She was twenty-seven years old at the time with beautiful brown hair and soft green eyes. She'd been taking care of our farm for the last six months or so while we had been gone. While we'd been at hospitals in Chicago and Atlanta for cancer treatment and then in Indiana when the treatments had stopped working.

Hopie had made trips to Indiana every chance she could, for as long as she could, to be with Joey. Some trips she made with Heidi, and some alone, by herself. Once she stayed for a month. Helping with Indiana. Helping with Joey.

But that was in the past now, and we were all at home, back in the farmhouse in Tennessee. Everyone except Joey. Through the kitchen window I could see the field and the cemetery where her wooden cross stood.

"Is there anything you want to tell me?" I asked. Hopie was sitting in the seat at the table where her mother always sat. To the right of mine. The kitchen, just like the house, was clean, and fresh flowers were on the table. All Hopie's doing. She wanted things to be just right when we got home.

"No," she answered. Her smile as big and kind as ever.

Hopie has a special gene in her that the rest of us weren't given. She is filled with joy all the time. Even when she is upset or heartbroken or scared . . . she radiates joy like no one I've ever known. From the time she was little, Hopie would brighten every room she walked into. Always rooting for the underdog and the misunderstood, she loved everyone the same, no matter who you were or where you were from.

In my first book I talked about how strong she is. How much weight she carries on her shoulders without anyone ever knowing and how she keeps her feelings inside. So deep that at times even she doesn't know what she's feeling or how to respond. Without me knowing it, that weight was about to come crashing down along with a bunch of feelings that I never even knew were there.

"Are you sure?" I asked again. Her right leg crossed over her left, nervously wiggling back and forth (a Feek habit all of us have).

"What are you asking for, Dad?" she answered, her smile only slightly fading.

"The truth, Hopie," I said. "Just tell me."

Her eyes started getting red, and tears started to fall. A big, big deal for Hopie, who almost never cries. Her hands were shaking now, and a lifetime of secrets were upon her.

"You won't understand," she answered through her tears. "You'll judge me."

"Just tell me, Hopie," I said again. "It's okay."

And she did.

She told me that her friend Wendy is more than just her friend. And that they had been dating for almost a year. And she was in love.

I'm not sure what I was expecting her to say, but I wasn't expecting that. A tear started to fall from my eye now.

"See, you're judging me," she said. And without even knowing I was, I was. She could see it on my face, see it in my eyes.

"I wasn't gonna tell you right now," she said, "you've been through so much." Immediately turning her pain to compassion for me and for Joey.

What happened next, I'm not really sure. We talked. We talked for a long time. I said some things I shouldn't have said. Reacting. Trying not to react.

The worst of it all, though, was my first reaction. My gut feelings down deep inside. Didn't she understand that I had a two-year-old baby, for God's sake, and I had just spent the drive home from Indiana and the last five months before that thinking about how I was going to need to protect the baby now more than ever? From hurt. From pain. From sin.

My conservative Christian faith was the first part of me to judge Hopie. To want to push her away. To withhold love from her. And she could feel it. See it in my eyes. And in that moment we had a conversation without any words.

Am I still going to get to be . . ., her eyes asked, *around my baby sister?* It's the question that she was probably the most worried about. That, and *Will you . . . still love me?*

My eyes were hardening around the edges, just like my heart.

Probably not, they said, as I looked away. More ashamed of what I was thinking than of what she had shared with me.

A few minutes later she went her way, and I went mine. I was shocked, and then again I wasn't. I had had a dream in Indiana. A dream about this. Or something close to it. And I had called Heidi and asked her about it. And being the big sister she is, she said I didn't have anything to worry about. Looking back now, I see she was protecting Hopie. And me. Hopie because this is not how I needed to find out about something so important. And me because I had enough on my plate to worry about at that moment. That was in the last two weeks before Joey passed away and our hearts and minds were working full-time just to process all that was happening there, let alone what might be happening somewhere back at home.

I put it out of my mind. Sort of. I returned to Joey's side and pretty much stayed there until the drive home two weeks later and the following funeral here at the farm. But it had stayed with me. In the back of my mind. While I held Joey's hand and she took her last breath, and it followed us home in the truck that night when we made the long, cold drive from Indiana to Tennessee.

And here we were. And there it was. The truth.

The truth that she could not . . . that she would not . . . tell her mother. No matter what. Hopie wouldn't hurt or scare her, and it would've been a lot for Joey to process there at the end. It would've been tough on her anytime, but in those last months and weeks, it probably would've been especially hard.

And so Hopie kept the truth to herself, just like she always had. Sometime during that time at the kitchen table, she told me about how she and Wendy had met and how there had been other girls. Other relationships. But she never told Joey and me. Instead, she went along with us rooting for her to marry our friend's older brother or date some guy that she and we knew wasn't right for her, for different reasons.

I can honestly say that in all those years before this, it had never occurred to us. To Joey and me. Not really. That doesn't mean we didn't think about all the possibilities of why Hopie was so awkward around boys when she was younger and was awkward still even in her twenties. But we never seriously gave it a moment of thought. We just kept praying that God would send her the right man, someone who would treat her well and love her for who she is.

And He did. Only it wasn't a man. It's Wendy.

On our anniversary this year, Hopie called me. I was pulling into a restaurant to have breakfast with two of my buddies after dropping off Indy at school, and my cell phone rang.

"Hold on, guys, it's Hopie . . . she's calling to wish me happy anniversary," I told them. And she was. And she wasn't.

"Guess what?" she said with so much excitement in her voice she sounded like she was in the car with me. "Wendy asked me to marry her . . ."

Silence.

No, actually there wasn't silence. I loved her too much to do that to her.

"Congratulations, honey!" I said. "I'm so happy for you." And the truth is, I was. And I am still.

A lot has happened in the year and a half between those conversations.

There's been some growth and some *aha* moments. Mostly on my end. We've had some hard conversations. A dinner once, where I asked Wendy about her past and what her plans were for the future. I fired questions at her for an hour, and she answered each one honestly and sincerely.

"I love your daughter," she said. And she did. I could see it in her eyes. And she is a good person. No, she's a great person. She's not kind and good just to Hopie, she's that way with everyone. And theirs is, strangely, a normal relationship. Hopie is the emotionally secure one in the relationship, and she encourages Wendy not to hold things in and to get out of her comfort zone. Wendy encourages Hopie to be more than she thinks she is. To be all that God made her to be.

Hopie is a Christian. She loves God and wants to honor Him. The same way she wants to honor Joey and me. But if you ask her about the rules of the church and their stance on people who are gay or lesbian, she will be quick to tell you, she doesn't agree. Just like she'd be the first person to stand up for a little girl with Down syndrome when other kids try to tell her she's less than they are.

Hopie has made me rethink everything I've ever thought when it comes to some things. And in other ways I'm still right where I always was. First off, I'm not the judge. That is not my job. I'm Hopie's father. My job is to love her. She gets to make her decisions in life. All of them. I can approve or disapprove, but it's her life, and she has a right to live it as she chooses.

And as far as the church goes, I am not the judge there either. My faith says that it's wrong. That it's wrong for me. And so I will live my life trying to live what I believe. But Hopie's faith is her faith. It is between her and God and no one else. You and I can try to judge her and condemn her or anyone else, but, honestly, we don't have any right to cast the first stone. At least, I don't. Not with all the stones I've thrown in my life.

And so we are going to have a wedding here at the farm. Around Halloween is what I hear. And I'm going to be excited about it. It will be a special day for someone who is special to me and her someone special. That is all I need to know.

I choose to love her. To love them. Period. End of story.

One Plus One

. . . sometimes equals a thousand.

It was the spring of 1988, and I had just returned from six months of an overseas deployment in Japan and had been away from my baby daughter Heidi for more than half a year and was so excited to be home.

When the Marine Corps shipped me out to Iwakuni, an American air base in the southern part of Japan, Heidi was nine months old. When I got back, she was almost a year and half. I had missed her terribly, and all I wanted to do was spend time with her and play catch-up on being a daddy.

The last thing I wanted to do was have another baby. Especially because Heidi's mom and I weren't doing so well. It wasn't that things were terrible, they just weren't great. And I'm not sure that she, nor I, were positive that this was going to last. Still, we were hopeful and had no plans to make any big changes in our life.

It turns out that God did, though.

"Congratulations, you're pregnant," the doctor said.

We were in Charleston, South Carolina, an hour's drive from the Marine air base where I was stationed at the time. We tried to act happy when we got the news, and in some ways we were, but another part of us was just caught off guard.

"Are you sure?" I asked. It didn't take a clinic full of doctorate diplomas on the wall to know that he was.

The drive home and the weeks that followed found me heavy in thought. I was nervous about having another child. At least, having one right then. We had issues of our own to work on, and I was just starting to get used to being a father to one little one. I selfishly didn't want to have to divide my time between two. I didn't want to divide my love. Thankfully, though, I didn't have to.

Not long after that, a friend told me something that I've never forgotten. "When a second child is born (or a third, etc.)," she said, "a parent's love doesn't get divided . . . it multiplies." And she was right. That is exactly what happened.

When Hopie came into this world, my heart was like the Grinch's on Christmas Day. It grew what seemed to be ten sizes larger. Hopie didn't get a portion of the love that I had left over from loving her sister, Heidi; she got a whole new batch of love that seemed to magically appear in our lives the morning she did.

Born Sarah Hope Feek, the little girl we've always called "Hopie" is almost thirty years old now, and I cannot imagine a life without her in it. So smart and beautiful and kind and full of love. Just like I can't imagine one without Heidi or their baby sister, Indiana. They are what makes life *life* for me. I live for their names to show up on my cell phone and for the evenings we get to share dinner together at our kitchen table. When they dance to the "Hokey Pokey" in the living room with their baby sister. And I hear them sing her to sleep at night . . . me parked on the bottom step of the stairway that leads up to her room and mine, listening and grinning ear to ear.

Thinking back to the time when Hopie was born, I am reminded about how worried Heidi was when Joey and I got the news that we were going to have a baby. Heidi was beyond upset. Even though she was in her late twenties and a grown woman, inside was a little girl who was scared.

A part of her was afraid that our love was going to be divided. That Joey and I might love her less and the new child more because she was going to be a part of both of us.

I remember Joey and I holding her as she cried and me telling Heidi the story about how love doesn't get divided; it only multiplies. And magically, just like with Hopie, it happened again.

Heidi, like Hopie, loves Indiana so much, they can hardly stand it. Like I live to see and hear from them, they live to see the baby's face on FaceTime or a new video or picture of her coming in via text from her papa.

Life is funny like that. What scares us most, in the end, brings us the most joy.

Joey is the ultimate example of that in our family. She didn't want kids. Didn't want to be a mama at all. Ever. The math didn't add up for her. Too much pain, time, responsibility, hassle, work, etc. . . . you name it. The numbers didn't work. And, of course, they don't. Having a baby probably always sounds bad on paper. But the magic of it is when they come. Then the numbers flip. You suddenly have more time, patience, energy, understanding, and especially . . . love.

Joey loved being a wife and a daughter and a friend and all the other roles she played in her life, but the role she loved most . . . was being a mother.

I am the same way. I suspect every parent is.

My College Years

Four years of living, loving, and learning.

I made one visit to a college in high school. It was a fall trip to Western Kentucky University, an hour or two away from Greenville, Kentucky, where my family was living at the time, and I was in my last year of school when we boarded the big yellow bus headed to Bowling Green. A couple of the teachers were taking the seniors there to watch a play. Something from Shakespeare that I don't remember much about. The thing I remember, though, was that some of the kids on the bus were going to college the next year. A number of them, to the school that we were visiting. They already had it all planned out. Others had the scholarships and grants in place to attend other colleges in other places around the state and country. That was the first time I'd even heard of any mention of college.

I remember sitting on the bus as we pulled up to that beautiful campus, thinking, *How do you go to college?* I had no clue, and no one had bothered to tell me.

Unfortunately, I was part of the group of kids that doesn't go to college, that never even thinks about universities and degrees. We go to trade schools or into the army. Or to prison. We get wives or girlfriends or both and have babies. That's how we spend our college years.

Years later I would find out that I could've gone to college. Easy. Almost on a free ride. Not because I was smart or super talented at sports or academics. But because we were poor. The poorest kind of poor. And my mother was raising five of us on nothing. That alone would've qualified me for every grant and loan under the sun.

But nobody told me. I felt like the main character in the movie *Rudy*. His dream was to go to Notre Dame, but the priest who was taking the kids to visit told him, "Not everyone is born to go to Notre Dame." That he was more of a "Holy Cross Junior College" kind of student. Less than the other kids. Way less.

I was probably a bit less than that. Seeing as how no one made any mention of junior or community colleges that might be right for me.

And so I didn't go to college. I went into the Marine Corps instead.

I spent my freshman year of college being yelled at and belittled by four Parris Island drill instructors. Then learning how to fix little black electronic boxes at a naval base north of Memphis. Then around what would have been my sophomore year, I was transferred to El Toro, a Marine air base on the West Coast. I guarded flight lines during the day, and since I still wasn't old enough to drink legally, I bought a fake ID so I could chase the California girls in the bars at night.

I caught one and we got married and shipped off to South Carolina. And we had a baby.

While other kids my age were making plans for graduation, I was stuffing a duffel bag full of uniforms and cowboy boots, about to do a six-month deployment to Japan. During the half year or so that I spent in Iwakuni, I would drink a hundred cases of beer, play music in the enlisted and officers' clubs on the base at night, and be anything but married. Even though I was.

It was during this time that I also started working out and would gain thirty pounds of muscle and go from being incredibly skinny my whole life, to not so skinny. My confidence soared, and my character plummeted. I was doing all I could to find happiness . . . but real peace, and real joy, eluded me. It would elude me for another ten years, and then slowly, and in an instant, everything would change—when I finally learned to let go of my death grip on life's steering wheel and let God do the real driving.

When the men and women from the class of '82 graduated from colleges with their sheepskin diplomas in hand and were just beginning to figure out where they wanted to go next and how best to start their lives . . . across the ocean at a base in Kaneohe Bay, Hawaii, mine was nearly over. Within a year or so, my checklist of things accomplished would have already included: married, divorced, and a single dad of two kids—all by the time I was twenty-five.

Don't get me wrong, I don't have any bad feelings about not going to college. It is what it is. Just like it was what it was. I have been given a wonderful life and wouldn't hardly have changed a thing, knowing now how blessed I would be. But, still, a part of me wonders what if? What if I'd grown up in a different family? With less welfare from the government and more than one parent looking out for the welfare of us five kids? I can't help but think about what I'd have done if I'd gone to college. Who I'd have become.

The truth is that I actually did go to college. Sort of. When I was stationed in Hawaii, a university out of Texas offered a program where I could take college courses at night and earn a degree. I took some classes and got an associate's degree, or that's what they said it was. But it has never come in handy for a single thing in my life. It never helped me get a job or not get one. Maybe it's because it wasn't a real degree. Probably it's because that teacher who talked to Rudy and the ones who didn't talk to me were right. I wasn't meant to go to college. I was meant for something better than that.

Joey never went to college either. She wasn't a fan of it. Or at least the idea that when every kid gets out of high school, they should go to college. That never made any sense to her. It makes no sense to me either. It seems like if you want to be a nurse or a teacher or an engineer or something like that, it's a given . . . you need to go. You have to, to make your dreams happen. But if you want something more than that or something less, then maybe there's another route.

When our two older daughters got out of school, we promised that we would pay for one year of college for each of them. From there, if they wanted to keep going, they'd have to figure it out. Neither of them did. Looking back, I'll bet they'll say the same thing that we do, that college isn't for everyone. That there are more good options out there, than just college.

Honestly, I look back on my college years fondly. I had some of the most amazing teachers, who weren't teachers, around me during those years, and I learned a ton about life and love . . . by doing. By making decisions and making mistakes. At times, those years seemed like an eternal spring break, mixed with a boatload of cramming to just keep up. Just to keep from getting expelled from life.

My real graduation probably came around 2000 or so, when I put the bottle down for a while and picked up a Bible. That's the moment when I started wanting more of myself than who and what I'd been. Those are things they couldn't have taught me at WKU or any other university or school. They are lessons that only life can teach. And I am thankful for them.

Semper Fi

Technically, I was given an honorable discharge
when I got out of the Marine Corps.
Unfortunately, almost thirty years
later, I don't feel much honor in it.

I had been in the service for eight years. Had reenlisted after four and was
a sergeant for the last three. I was good at my job and had done my duty
well, I think, at least most of it. All but the part at the end.

It was December 1990 when my discharge papers came in. Our country wasn't at war, but it was close to it. I was about to miss the whole thing.
That wasn't the reason I was getting out or that they were letting me out
a little bit early, but it was a fact.

I had been stationed in Kaneohe Bay, Hawaii, and I left the air station
on a plane in late December, headed to civilian life in Texas. Within a
month or so most of my buddies got on planes, but they were headed to
Bahrain. A small island nation somewhere in the Persian Gulf. A blink
later Desert Storm happened. I watched on TV like most of the world. My
friends, the ones who had to leave their families and do their duty during
wartime, saw it firsthand.

My job was to repair broken little black boxes from airplanes. They were electronic components in camera systems for F-4 Phantoms and F-18 Hornets—jets that Marine pilots flew and my unit helped keep in the air.

I had gone to basic training in Parris Island, then electronic school in Millington, Tennessee. Spent almost a year there the first time, then came back a few years later for another year of advanced electronic courses in '88. They taught us how to run tests and fix the broken units that came in, but I had no idea how electricity worked. I still don't. If I want to add a plug in Joey's garden shed, I google it when I get to Home Depot, and YouTube tells me what to do.

It's strange that you can learn so much and not know anything. I think the problem was that I learned a lot of high-level technician stuff but was never taught the low-level basics that go with it. I wasn't fixing airplanes, I was fixing boxes. We never spent any time around the aircraft unless it was to walk the flight line with a gun or pick up loose gravel, so the big picture of what we were doing eluded me. Just like the big picture of what I was doing in life did.

When the girls' mom and I split up, and ultimately when Hopie came back to live with Heidi and me, we had to make our family. A new one out of what was left. And we were trying to. But there were issues. The Marine Corps needed a backup plan. To know that if I got a call in the middle of the night that Uncle Sam needed me in Iraq or somewhere else, I could ship out at a moment's notice and my girls would have someone to take care of them. I didn't have that.

A nearby pastor and his wife offered to keep Heidi and Hopie, but I didn't know them that well and wasn't comfortable letting that happen. So I called my mom, who was living in either Texas or Florida at the time, and she said she would come. The plan was for her to live with us in Hawaii where I was stationed . . . that she would get an extended vacation in paradise and I would have a backup plan for the kids. It was a win-win for everyone, especially the kids, who were excited to have their grandmother around for a while.

So she caught a plane and was soon walking beside us down Waikiki Beach, all of us picking up shells and making plans for what would happen if I was to get called away . . . which had a pretty good chance of happening since Iraq had just invaded Kuwait not long before.

Mom's time in Hawaii lasted a week. Two weeks tops. Not because she didn't love the girls or me or didn't want to be there to help but because she didn't like the girl I was seeing at the time. She took one look at her and decided she was ready to fly back to the mainland.

It wasn't the girl, though, honestly. It was me that Mom didn't approve of. The girl was just an excuse. She had come to Hawaii married and separated with her husband and was shacked up with the girls and me. She still had her own place, but she might as well have been living with us.

Mom was on a plane headed back east shortly after. And I was there with a hot girlfriend who was technically still married to some other guy and no backup plan. The girlfriend as a backup plan wasn't an option either for some reason. In hindsight, I should have wondered why.

However, it worked out that the Marines decided if I couldn't come up with a backup plan for my kids, they'd come up with a backup plan for me. A month or two later I was on a plane headed to Texas, and someone else was inbound from the states to take my place.

I've not told this story before. Not for any particular reason. It's no worse or better than a lot of other crappy stories from my past. It's just one, I guess, I mostly forgot about. And, somehow, taking a pen and poking at the past seems to wake up sleepy memories like this one.

When I got out of the service, the girl I was seeing flew to Texas with me and Heidi and Hopie, and she and my mother became friends, sort of. We got an apartment in Dallas, and not long after, Mom decided not to come visit us there either. Not because of the girl this time, but because we wouldn't let her smoke in the apartment. This was in the early '90s, and the country was a million miles from where they are now with smoking. Nonsmokers were freaks at the time and treated with disrespect, at least I was.

In the end, again, it wasn't just the cigarettes that Mom had a problem with. It was probably me. She was disappointed in the boy she had raised.

I'm not sure if it ever occurred to her that most of these terrible decisions I was making with regard to love and life were pretty much exact replicas of decisions she had made when us kids were growing up with her.

And Mom wasn't the only one disappointed in me. I was too. I knew better. I knew that I knew better, and yet I couldn't stop myself from touching the flame . . . even though I was well aware that it was gonna burn me.

I was in the service from 1982 to 1990 and served during peacetime. The Reagan era. I was even part of the guard unit that stood post when President Reagan came to South Carolina to speak one time. I look back with pride on that day but not on most of those years.

As I mentioned, I was a pretty good Marine when I was in. At the top, or near the top, of my class in NCO school and pretty much any other training I had. And, at times, with the medals on my chest, I even looked a little like a poster-boy Marine. But inside, my Semper Fi was in question.

The phrase *Semper Fi* is Latin, and we first learned it in boot camp. It means "always faithful." It is the Marine Corps motto. But it's not always the motto of the Marines who wear the uniform. It is something that is much easier to say than do. To claim, rather than live up to the name.

I didn't understand the power of it then. Those words. What they mean. But I do now. And though I was given an honorable "hardship" discharge when I got out of the service, I would have many, many more hardships ahead of me. And, in time, I would be the last person to ask for or expect special treatment when they came along. Instead, I would realize, just as I understand now . . . that it is in the hard things of life—the difficulties—that we grow. That we get the chance to stretch our character and be molded a little bit more like Christ and a little bit less like ourselves.

I wore my old Marine uniform for the first time in a long time this past Saturday night. Believe it or not, it still fits me. Not the same way—the chest is a little looser and the belly a bit tighter—but it fits. It was for a 1960s-themed surprise birthday party for our middle daughter, Hopie. She and her sister wore go-go boots and short dresses and their hair in bouffant. I had the name "GUMP" written in Sharpie on a piece of masking tape above the left pocket, just over the Marine Corps emblem. I told them that Indy in her little blue vintage dress was Jenny and I was Forrest Gump when he was in the army. "We get it, Dad," the girls smiled and said. They always love to see me in my uniform.

It's funny to put it on after all these years. My back gets a little straighter and my chest puffs up a bit and my walk has some swagger to it. All because of a uniform. And the pride I felt wearing it. That I feel wearing it still.

I've learned that nobody cares about what kind of discharge papers we got thirty years ago, they care about who we are now. The honor that we show others. And how faithful we are to our friends and to the ones we love. I'm so thankful that I got the chance to learn what Semper Fi means when I was with Joey. What it really means to love someone and honor them with every part of your being. It might have taken me a while to truly understand it—between hearing it the first time in boot camp in 1982 and marrying Joey in 2002 . . . twenty years—but I didn't just say it, I meant it, and I lived it out. I'm living it out now. Still.

Better late than never.

Barber Shopping

For our whole marriage, Joey is the
only one who ever cut my hair. Ever.

Every two and a half weeks or so for the past fourteen years, I'd sit in a chair in our bathroom and my wife would pull out the clippers and a pair of scissors and do her best to make her man look his best. I think she did a great job, especially with what she had to work with. Me.

I don't think Joey ever cut hair before she started cutting mine. Except maybe her brother Justin's in high school, when he wanted a buzz cut and all she had to do was run some tight clippers over it a few times and was done. I, on the other hand, was an expert on haircuts, sort of. I had been in the service, sitting in a barber's chair watching someone cut my hair once a week for eight years whether it needed it or not. And though I had no idea how to actually cut hair, I had a pretty good idea how other people cut mine. And so right about the time we got married, Joey and I bought some clippers and proceeded to challenge our marriage like never before.

I was a bit of a perfectionist. At times I still can be. And so she had her work cut out for her. I'm not sure who was more nervous the first few times she cut it . . . her or me. It probably took an hour and a half that first haircut, but by the time we hit the ten-year mark, I'd be in and out of the chair in twenty minutes. Maybe less.

She loved cutting my hair, and I loved that she didn't mind doing it. First off, I think she liked that we were saving money by her doing it, and, secondly, she took pride in it. It was just one more way to serve her husband. To love him greatly. I liked it because I never had to leave home to get my hair cut . . . and I got to feel up my barber while she cut my hair (just kidding . . . actually, I'm not). We would laugh and talk and just be together while she snipped and clipped. It was quiet time for us, when we locked the world outside the door, and it was just her and me and a bunch of blondish-red hair falling to the floor.

I'll bet I have dozens of different haircuts she gave me on film. A camera running while the clippers buzzed and the scissors snipped. It is surreal to watch those clips now. Because it isn't like we were capturing a big moment in our lives. Us going up on stage to win an award or a special family dinner. It was just a mundane task that she would do and I had to get done. But I think that's why those video clips are so special. Because they are life. They are our lives in a nutshell. And when you see Joey standing over me with my hair in her fingers, measuring . . . through the doorway of the kitchen . . . there's something beautiful about it. She was so alive. Our love so alive.

Joey continued cutting my hair through thick and thin. She cut it on tour buses and in green rooms at concert venues. At her mama's house and in hotel bathrooms. One time she even cut it in the parking lot of the Bill Clinton Memorial Library in Little Rock, Arkansas. We were on tour with Don Williams, and that evening's show had been canceled, so Russ parked our bus in that big parking lot, and Joey brought out a chair and her clipper set and let 'er fly. We must have been quite a sight—me, all wrapped up under a plastic robe, and Joey, scissors in one hand and comb in the other. Right next to a great big tour bus with our pictures ten feet high on the sides of it.

And when the cancer came back a second time and Joey got sick, she kept cutting my hair. At least until she couldn't cut it anymore. Then I just stopped getting it cut altogether.

I remember we were at her mama's farmhouse in Indiana and had been there for a month or so, and my hair was easily more than a month past due for being cut. And Joey kept mentioning to me that I needed to go somewhere and get it cut. I told her that I was just gonna wait till she got better and have her cut it then. That was true, but another reason was that no one else had cut my hair, and I didn't want to give up hope that wasn't going to have to change. Besides, her hair had pretty much all fallen out when she had me run the clippers over it, and not long after, her sisters and daddy and best friend all cut their hair in support of her and in defiance of the disease that was trying to take her down. I had decided not to cut mine for the same reason. She didn't get to be the best her during that time, and I had no intention of being the best me either. I was adamant not to cut my hair until Joey could do it, if ever.

The situation finally came to a head sitting beside her bed one afternoon. We had recently received another heartbreaking round of bad news and it was looking like it was only a matter of time now before the cancer was going to take her. "Please go get your hair cut, honey," she said. Then she followed it up with a sentence I didn't expect to hear. With all the sincerity in the world, she looked at me and said, "This is not how I want to remember you."

Remember me? I thought. *That's not how it works. I'm the one who's supposed to remember you.* I couldn't help but smile great big.

A week or two later she had a reprieve and started feeling better. She even got up from her bed and was able to walk from room to room with her walker and morphine drip in tow.

"Go get my clippers," she said. And I knew she was feeling better.

My sister-in-law filmed that haircut too. It's precious. Joey barely ninety pounds, I'll bet, her body full of cancer . . . still loving being a wife to her husband. That was my last haircut before she passed away.

When I got back here to Tennessee and we started getting ready for Joey's funeral service, I had a small list of things that she'd asked me to do. Make sure we had her dress and jean jacket ready, which song she wanted our friend Bradley Walker to sing at the service, and where she wanted me to go get my haircut.

She knew I was still going to be resistant to the idea, so she had me write down her wishes: go to the square in downtown Columbia and tell Daniel, who runs the barbershop there, that this was a special occasion and for him to do his best to cut it like she did.

And so that's just what I did. The funeral was on a Tuesday, so I called him the morning before and had to leave a voice message on the shop's machine because they were closed on Mondays. He called me back right away and opened his shop, special for me.

When I sat down in his chair, I told him what she had said, and tears fell from his eyes, just like they fell from mine. Daniel has a big burly handlebar mustache, so I'm guessing he's not much of a crier, but that day he was. When he finished, he spun me around to face the mirror and asked, "How's it look?" "Perfect," I answered without even looking. And it was. The moment was just as Joey had wanted.

Since that day I have had a bunch of haircuts. By a number of different people. Daniel another time or two, another fella in his shop, and also some girls and guys in other barbershops and salons from Chapel Hill to Cool Springs. One of them was more than fifty dollars for the haircut, when you include the expected tip, and another was five bucks, and she refused to let me leave a tip. But no matter the price, they always end up the same. Me disappointed. Trying not to show it.

It's not that the haircuts are bad . . . most have been pretty good, though, from time to time, they're a little rough. I'm mostly disappointed that someone else has to cut it at all. That my wife isn't here to do it. Or to opt not to if she wants.

A few months ago I opened the small wooden cabinet in the bathroom and pulled out our old clippers. The ones that Joey used to cut my hair all those years. And I pulled in a chair from the kitchen and sat down and gave myself the best Joey haircut I could. And you know what, it wasn't much different than the ones I've been getting from other folks who cut hair for a living. Except for one major thing. It happened at home, like she used to cut it. And for whatever it's worth, it was comforting to me.

This coming weekend I'm supposed to be playing a show across the driveway in our concert hall, and I'm in dire need of a haircut again. I'm not sure if I'll head to town after porch time on Wednesday and see if Daniel or someone will give me a trim or if I'll just do it myself. One thing's for certain, though. It doesn't really much matter.

The only person I am wanting to impress isn't here.

Choo-Choo Training

. . . parenting in Pampers.

I'm in the middle of potty training Indy. She calls it "choo-choo" training. And she's not far off because most of the time, as she's sitting on her little potty chair, I'm sitting beside her on the floor of the bathroom thinking, *I know you can, I know you can, I know you can . . .*, and then when there's success, it's more like, *. . . I knew you could, I knew you could.*

Even though I went through this twenty-something years ago with Heidi and Hopie, for the most part, this is all brand-new to me. Either I wasn't around much when Heidi and Hopie were potty training, or I just can't remember how we did it. So I am having to read blogs and ask friends the best way to teach her to ditch the Pampers and go "like a big girl."

Fortunately, I have some wonderful neighbor ladies around me who are jumping in and helping with ideas and advice and even activities to make this time more fun for Indiana. And we're getting there. On a dry-erase board that hangs on the wall in the bathroom above Indy's potty chair is a weekly chart, divided up into days . . . with dozens of pink and blue stickers placed in not-so-straight rows by Indy every time she has success. Each sticker represents a hug and a high five and lots of excitement here at our house.

I have only been working with Indy consistently on it for the last two weeks, but Joey started potty training Indy early on. I have videos of Joey sitting beside her on the floor and reading books to Indy as she sat on a little wooden potty chair when she was less than a year old. And Joey kept doing that daily for almost the next whole year until life caught up with us and our days became filled with more pressing concerns. Because Joey worked with Indy so long, she is picking up the idea pretty quickly. Her main problem is still her core strength. Though she's walking, she's still a little unstable and won't bend her legs much, so getting on and off the potty by herself isn't easy for her to do. But little by little, she's getting there.

I know that before too long this training will be behind us, and I'll look back and laugh at the process we're going through. But, right now, it's tough to laugh when Indy gets off the potty and I put her in the bathtub for a bath and within two minutes she's got a new "toy" floating around in the bath with her that I didn't put there.

I think she knows what she's doing. She's trying to outlast me, and so far it's working. But I can be pretty stubborn, and, in the end, I'm committed to throwing away all the diapers in the next few months. Or at least that's what my goal is. I have learned that sometimes you have to adjust . . . the time frame we have in mind to make big changes in our lives may not be realistic.

Learning to be a parent again . . . at least learning how to be a good one is very similar. I just want to put my big-boy pants on and be as great of a father as I believe my wife would've been as a mother, but it's not that easy. I'm gonna make some mistakes. Sometimes they are little ones that clean up easy, and some of them are all-out messes.

I sent Indiana to school one day in a swimsuit that I thought was a cute jumper outfit (note to self . . . don't Instagram these kinds of moments), and everyone got quite a kick out of it. When I came to pick her up at the end of the day, the teacher looked at me, giggling, and said, "You know that's a swimsuit, right?" I tried to play it off, like, "Yeah, of course . . . ," trying to act confident in my choice, like if it were to rain that day, she'd be ready for it. But both the teacher and I knew that I was still new at this and had some training of my own to do.

Sometimes it's a little bit bigger mess that I make, like what's happening now. Somehow, she's picked up the bad habit of chewing her nails (her poor little nails are worn down to the nub because she chews on them so much), and I am constantly telling her not to do that. But she just looks at me like I'm from Mars. And it's usually right about then that I'll realize that as I'm saying it, my hand is in my mouth, and I'm chewing on my own nails. That one isn't so easy to fix.

But like her potty training, I'm setting some goals to be a better daddy. A better papa, actually. And if I stay consistent and keep trying . . . sooner or later, I won't have to wait for someone to high-five me every time I do something right; it'll just be what comes naturally. It will happen without having to think about it at all.

In the meantime you'll find me sitting beside our little one on the bathroom floor, reading books about *Five Little Ducks* and how *Corduroy Goes to the Doctor* until magic happens and we get to stand up bare-butted and pick out another sticker for the wall.

Dollars and Sense

Money can't buy Hopie's happiness.

"Is that a lot?" Hopie asked when we were all gathered at the kitchen table and had just opened an envelope full of "mailbox money" from ASCAP for a song I had written that was just a big old hit on the radio.

The check was for six digits. Over a hundred thousand dollars. Joey and I and our oldest daughter, Heidi, were in awe, staring at it, not hardly believing that much money could be made by writing some words that rhyme on a piece of paper. Hopie wasn't sure what we were so excited about. She asked again, "Is that a lot?"

That might not seem like a big deal, but it is when your middle daughter is sixteen years old and in high school. Most kids that age would know better than I would how much money that is.

"Yes, honey, it's a lot."

"That's great, Dad," is all she said. Smiling. Proud of me for doing whatever it was I had done to make enough money for us to pay our bills and then some.

Joey and I looked at each other, both thinking the same thing . . . *Thank You, Lord, for letting Hopie still be so innocent.*

She was that way with time too. It could be March or mid-June, and we'd be talking about Christmas, and Hopie would say, "Is that a long time away?" It's not that she couldn't sit down and figure out how many months it was between the spring and the winter. She just didn't care. It wasn't something that concerned her or she gave much thought to. It was the future. She was about the present. She always was. She is still.

I believe that's how she was with money also. It isn't that she couldn't stop and think about how many zeros were on that check and compare it to what the minimum wage was at the time . . . it's just that those kinds of things weren't important to her. They didn't matter. And to tell you the truth, they don't much matter to her now.

Hopie is great with money. Better than me, probably. But she doesn't care about it the way most people do. She cares that she has enough. That she can pay her bills and buy high-quality dog food for her overgrown puppy, Boulett. And that she can put some back for a rainy day. But she doesn't long to have a lot of it or to buy a lot of stuff. It's just not how she's wired. She gets that from her mama, I think. From Joey. She was the same way. Practical.

I love that about Hopie. And I love that she is her own person. Not better than anyone else or worse. Just herself. Who God has made her to be. She is the champion of underdogs and the lover of the unlovable. I'd like to tell you I am the same way, but I'm not. Maybe on my best day, I make an effort to be, but on her worst day, she's more like Jesus than I'll ever be.

She doesn't know that about herself, though. I think she only sees her flaws. The areas where she has fallen behind the other kids at school and never caught up. Even nearing thirty years old, she's still trying to measure up to the other kids who are thirty. At least, I worry that she is.

We all are, I guess. It's in all of us. The longing to be the same. To be accepted. But, honestly, I don't want Hopie to be the same. She somehow made it through a tough childhood with the best parts of her intact. The parts that the world shamed out of most of the rest of us years and years ago. But not Hopie. She is still innocent and naive. Filled with joy that is unshakable and love that she gives freely and that doesn't have to be returned to her. It is one of the things I am most proud about who she is. That she is so good, with nothing . . . and I mean nothing . . . but the best of intentions.

I'm not sure if Hopie will ever read this book. I'm not sure if she ever read my first one. I know she and Wendy were reading it out loud to each other for a while, but I'm not sure if she ever finished it. Or if she'll find time to work her way through this one. It doesn't really matter if she does or if she doesn't. She's part of this one and the last. Just like her sister Heidi is. They are part of me. Raising me to be who I am, just as I was trying to raise them to be who they have turned out to be.

Like Heidi and Hopie, I am still a work in progress. God isn't finished with me yet. I'm a mess and a miracle. A sinner who'll never be a saint. But I'm trying. Believing that the good can overcome the bad. That love always conquers fear. And it does. Even if it doesn't look like it does.

I'm not sure how many of these books I'll sell. Could be a good amount. Could be embarrassing . . . mostly to the publishers who printed it. But either way, at some point, I'll be at my kitchen table, and some sort of royalty check will come in. And I hope that Hopie is there. Here. And as I look at the zeros, whether there's a bunch of them or none at all . . . she will ask, "Is that a lot, Dad?"

And I'll smile and say, "Yes, honey, it sure is."

Unwritten

Life deleted.

My mother was a writer, or, at least, she wanted to be. She loved books and most mornings or evenings could be found with a cigarette in one hand and a novel in the other. Devouring stories by Ayn Rand, Dean Koontz, John Steinbeck, and many others. When I picture my mom in my mind, I think of her sitting at the kitchen table with a cup of coffee or a can of beer—reading. Always reading. The countertop at her house was always filled with books she'd read, that she was getting ready to read. She'd buy them at secondhand stores, check 'em out from the library, or pick them up at yard sales for a dime.

And Mom didn't just love to read, she loved to write. She filled journals for years and years with her thoughts and observations and wrote countless stories on the iMac computer that I had given her. She talked about writing a book one day. Dreamed about having her own book in the library or a yard sale for someone to find. And she had talent. From time to time she would read me something she was working on. Or put some words down in a card for my birthday. And you could tell it was there—the gift. We had countless conversations about writing, and I was always trying to encourage her to go for it. To tell her story. Or one that she had inside her and wanted to share.

But, in the end, no one has ever read her stories, and no one ever will. Because, for some reason, my mother made the decision to hit delete on all of her writings right before she passed away. And to throw away most of the journals and papers she wrote out by hand.

I've often wondered why Mom decided not to leave them behind. Maybe they were too personal. Written just for her and not for others to read. I'm guessing that must be it. But looking back—now that Mom has been gone for three years—I know all of us, my brothers and sisters and the grandkids, wish that she had more of her left here. More of her voice and her thoughts that could live on and more of her wisdom to share with us as we're trying to make our way through life.

Even though I'd like to think I knew my mother fairly well, the truth is that she is a mystery to me. Who she was . . . I mean who she *really* was. I guess I will never know. I know quite a bit about her. About her growing up in Michigan and her teenage years of rebellion and also some things about her marriage to my dad and also to my older brother's father. And I have the memories growing up with her and our lives together as they intersected through the years, but there is much more that I don't know about her. That I wish I knew.

Maybe that is why I'm a writer. I'm sure it's part of it. Her love for the written word was passed on to me, just like my father's love for country music was.

I can't imagine deleting my life's work, though. Part of my reason for writing anything, even the words I'm writing right now, is to share them. To have a record of my experiences and thoughts about life and to have a way to pass those on to my children and their children. And to lots of other people I'll never meet. With the hope that something in the words I write and stories I tell might be helpful to someone.

From time to time my mother would tell me about a certain book that she would say I needed to read. Not often. But now and then. She knew I wasn't a great reader. That it was a challenge for me to find or take time to sit and get into a novel. Besides, I was and am mostly a nonfiction guy. I love stories, but my favorites are the ones that are true. About real people and the lives they lived. My bookshelf is mostly filled with biographies. The stories of John Wooden, Abraham Lincoln, Norman Rockwell, and dozens of other people whose lives or work I have found interesting.

My mother's love of books intersected with my life deeply in the fall of 2001. I had turned an old hardware store in Mount Pleasant into a songwriting studio and was spending my days writing songs there when a woman came through the door one morning. She was a nurse who had been sent to give me a checkup for the life insurance company I had recently signed up with. I had not met her before, but she was very kind, and we chitchatted a bit as she took my blood pressure. Then she pointed to a book sitting on my desk.

"Have you read that?" she asked, her fingers aimed at the memoir *All Over but the Shoutin'* by Rick Bragg.

"No, not yet," I answered. "My mom gave it to me and said I might like it."

The lady just stared at me, then put her stethoscope down and touched my hand and said, "You need to read it."

I was a bit startled.

"Yeah, I'll try to, but I'm pretty—"

Before I could finish, she said, "Your mother needs you to read this book." And she just kept staring at me, like she wasn't going to let me up.

Now, this lady didn't know me or my mother, but I got the impression that she knew the book, and what was inside of it must have spoken to her.

"Okay, I'll read it."

The next day I was in a line waiting to walk into traffic court in Franklin and had the book in my hand. I had a parking ticket that I needed to pay, and as I was waiting for the doors to open, I started reading. Within a few pages, I was mesmerized. Hooked. Drawn deep into a story that cut me to the bone. There must've been fifty people in that line, but, all of a sudden, I was there all alone with the book. With this man's words about his mother and the things that she had been through for him. And for his brothers and his family. And as I read, my tears started falling. It wasn't just a great book, it was great writing. Some of the best I've ever read. And the way he told his story—her story—killed me. I was shaking. Sobbing so hard I could barely see the words as I stood in that line with a room full of strangers.

For the next two days, that book went with me everywhere. I would read a chapter and reread it. I had never done that before. I would read a line, then stop and think about it. Then move on to the next one.

It was easy to understand why that lady had wanted me to read it. Because it was an important story. And it wasn't just the author Rick Bragg's story, it was my story. Not just about his mother, it was about mine also. A tribute to any son or daughter's mother who went through hell trying to build a better life for her kids. My guess is that it was this lady's story or her mother's.

I ran into that lady in a restaurant a couple of weeks ago for the first time in the fifteen years or so since that day. I didn't remember her, but she remembered me.

"I gave you a physical in Mount Pleasant—," she started to say as she reached out for my hand. I cut her off.

"You told me about the book," I said.

"Yes, *All Over but the Shoutin'*." I was surprised that she remembered.

"Thank you, thank you so much," I said. And I stood by her table for the next ten minutes telling her how much it meant to me and why.

That day in 2001 and that book did two things for me, I think. First off, it forever changed how I looked at my mother. I mean, it completely changed how I related to this person I was so closely related to. Even though my mom had made doozies of mistakes when it came to raising us, it gave me permission to love her anyway and to lift her up high. It showed me how much I owed my mother—how much I owe her still.

The other thing that day and book did was inspire me. I am still a young writer. Not in age but in experience. But the benchmark for me is still that book. Those words on those pages. The truth that he wrote in black and white. The best of the best of a bad situation.

I have had a lot of time to think about that book and the impact it's made on me. And how, though my mother never wrote a book of her own or saved her writings for me to read, she shared her story with me . . . through that book. Or at least a part of it that she wanted and needed me to know and remember.

She may have hit delete on her computer, but in a way . . . her story remains.

Dearly Beloved

"Some people vow to keep their vow,
even when they don't have to."

Joey's mama didn't just make that vow in the late 1960s when she married Joey's daddy, she made it for life. No matter what.

Lots of folks do. Actually, I'm sure everyone does. But then, a lot of the time, something happens, and that vow loses its significance. And, instead of a vow, the words you said were more of a hope. A wish. Something that can be broken or changed if it doesn't work out the way you were thinking it would.

And I understand it because I've said it myself and moved on. Most of us have, unfortunately.

But Joey's mother, June, vowed those words and never moved on. Even when her husband, Jack, did. That doesn't make her or him worse or better than the other. It just makes her unique to me. I have always found June to be an amazing woman, and this is one of the things that sets her apart from most people I know.

When Joey's brother, Justin, died in a car accident at seventeen, it was hard on the family. Too hard. And when you couple that with a lot of issues that were already there, her parents' marriage came unraveled. They divorced, and Joey's daddy moved on. Found love and remarried. He and his new wife have been together fifteen years or so now and are doing well.

But June never moved on. She is still in the same farmhouse and committed in an unusual way to her ex-husband. She is friends with his new wife and has been for years and years. And family get-togethers with kids and grandkids are an open house where everyone is always welcome. She knows that she played a role in their relationship ending and she can't go back and change that. Or fix it. It is what it is. But she can take some responsibility for who she is today and the role she plays in the story she is telling with her life right now and in the future.

If you ask June why she has never dated someone else or fallen in love over the last almost twenty-five years since their divorce, she will be quick to give an answer: "I have to be available to take care of Jack if something happens to him." Now, that was the strangest thing to hear when she first shared it with me, but after hearing Joey's mama say it several times over a dozen years or so, I've come to realize that's just part of who she is. She wants to do the best right thing even if it makes no sense to the rest of the world. And even if he has moved on and someone else is first in line to take care of her ex-husband when he gets old and frail . . . she believes it's her responsibility if extra help is needed. And not in a "burden" sort of way. Like it's just an ordinary part of life.

I love that. That some people out there stay committed to someone or something even when they don't have to. It's a rare thing to come across that kind of commitment in the world today.

Fixer-Upper

Don't just stand there . . . do something stupid.

It made no sense to buy it. It was beyond run-down, and if it had potential, a slew of other folks who had looked at it first didn't see any. But, for some reason, I did. Maybe at the time I saw myself in that old broken-down farmhouse. Not just living in it someday. But that the house was in some ways similar to myself. A worn-out mess and broken beyond repair, without much hope. And I think I needed that old house just as much as it needed me.

Classic Greek revival in style, the house was built in the 1870s. I bought it in the summer of 1999 and spent two years fixing it up. Actually, I've spent almost twenty years fixing it up. But for the first two that's pretty much all I did from daybreak till dusk. Some mornings I'd be on a ladder scraping paint on the front of the house when the kids would get on the school bus, and I'd still be there when the bus dropped them off that afternoon.

I had no experience fixing up houses and no idea what I was doing (that is a constant theme that runs through this book and my life), but I believed I could figure it out. And so one of the first things I did was go to the Home Depot and buy their big "1-2-3" book. It was sort of a "how to fix up a house for dummies" manual. Unfortunately, even that was a bit over my head, but I did my best with it. I bought a bunch of tools and materials and was soon knee-deep in drywall and sawdust.

Like me, the house needed a complete overhaul, starting with the foundation. The far east corner, where the kitchen is, had a hard lean to it . . . easily six inches lower than the rest of the house. If you were making dinner and dropped a potato, you'd have to chase it across the floor till it stopped rolling and came to rest against the base of the counter. There were no real cabinets, just a sink on a basin, a stand-alone stove, and a water heater in the corner. We basically gutted the kitchen and started over, floor to ceiling. For the first month or so, there were no counters or sinks in the kitchen at all, so the kids and I washed all our dishes with a garden hose outside the back door.

Thankfully, I wasn't working on it all by myself all the time. I had some help at times. Some friends from Franklin or Nashville, who probably felt bad for me and the girls, would make the trip down and help me sand or paint or pull the worn-down layers of linoleum off the plywood that covered the hardwood floors. And at times when I could afford it, I hired professionals to do the really big stuff I knew I couldn't handle.

A team came in and shored up all the floors in the house. They were all like trampolines when you walked on them, especially upstairs. I think Heidi and Hopie found the bouncy floors amusing, but I didn't. Especially when I got the bill for the piers that were poured and the specialty-cut beams that were installed to reduce the "give" under each room's floor joists. Those bills were painful, but they were necessary. I soon learned that you can't just make something look pretty on the outside; it's gotta be solid all the way through, or you're gonna regret it.

Another team came in and redid the downstairs hardwood floors. The girls and I moved in with our neighbor Danny Potter and his wife, Carol, for a few days and came back home every afternoon to check our answering machine for any calls we missed. Since the rooms and floors had to be completely cleared, we ran the line for the phone and answering machine to a windowsill so we could drive over and stand outside, checking our messages every day without going inside.

The floors downstairs are beechwood. They were all covered with layers of linoleum and plywood underneath those. I'm guessing they covered the hardwood in the 1920s or '30s to make the house warmer in the winter, or maybe the linoleum just made the floors easier to keep clean. Either way, those layers helped save the wide planks that were underneath. When the polyurethane was dry and we got to come back in, I was in awe of how beautiful the floors were. They are still beautiful.

The other help I had was Heidi and Hopie, who were teenagers at the time. They pitched in where they could. For the first six months or so, we lived only downstairs, all together in one room, because the upstairs was in such bad shape. No one had lived up there in years and years, and the rooms looked like something out of a scary movie. Water damage everywhere, with ancient wallpaper covered in dead spiders hanging from the ceiling and walls.

I think the girls knew I was in over my head, but they rolled up their sleeves with me and scraped and prepped and did their best to see the potential in the house too. Honestly, I think if you asked the kids about it now, they'd tell you they thought I was crazy—buying that old house and us moving so far away from the apartment life in Nashville that we knew. They were sure it was a mistake. But they'll also be the first to tell you that it wasn't. That they love it so much now. They love what it's become and all it took to get there. So do I.

The girls love coming home to the farm. It's magical for them too. Not just how it looks or the transformation of the house and the barns around it. But how it's transformed our lives—theirs included. They see it just like I do. Just like Joey did. They were here and know firsthand the story that has unfolded in the rooms and on this land. They know the work I did—that Joey and I and they did—and they also know the things that we didn't do, that happened. The unexplainable providence that has been at work in our lives since buying this farm almost twenty years ago.

I'm thankful that our kids see the magic in this place too. Because one day this rural castle will be theirs. And it's important that they understand that the decisions we make—the ones we really make and follow through on—change everything. And that change will take you places you never dreamed.

For me, the value of the farmhouse and land we live on has nothing to do with what they're worth. Or how much the bank would loan us against it. I know that there are good reasons the world looks at a home that way, but what the resale value of our property is holds almost no bearing on what the real value of the home is. I can do the math, and when you take into account what we paid for the place, the nearly twenty years of improvements we've made to it (and are still making now), and what the land value is like locally right now, it clearly won't add up to be a good deal. One plus one in this case equals "I'm an idiot." But I don't care. For me, the math is completely different with a different set of rules than what I learned in my grade school math book.

How do you put a price tag on the memories you make? On the years of laughter you've shared and the tears of heartbreak you've cried? Or the dreams that have come true because you chose to live there? When I start to add up those things on my brain's calculator . . . we stole this place. We won the lottery and got it for a song.

As a matter of fact, just outside the window here by my recliner, as I'm writing this right now, there's the crunching and beeping sounds of heavy machinery scraping dirt and getting the drive ready for asphalt. We just poured concert pads, and now the whole long stretch of driveway is about to go from the dirt and gravel mix that it's always been . . . to asphalt. It's a ridiculous amount of money to have it done, but I'm so excited, I can hardly stand it.

I can't see the dollar signs. All I can see is the little girl on a tricycle who is gonna ride back and forth and round and round and say, "Papa, Papa . . . look," as she pushes on the pedals and makes the big wheel in the front turn. I know, I know . . . that's an expensive tricycle path, and yes, it is. Crazy expensive. But that's only because I don't know all the difference it's going to make yet. The good part isn't what I can see in front of me, it's the part we can't see. The unknown.

I can't really ask our business manager for advice on this one because I know what she'll say. That it doesn't make sense . . . and something about depreciating value and return on investment . . . but that is all Greek to me. Let me just do a little bit of the math for you, and you'll see what I mean.

Raised two wonderful daughters here. Got married here. Built a beautiful life here . . . priceless. Built a music career from scratch, TV programs from our barn . . . priceless. Had a new baby at home . . . priceless. My wife (and my mother) are buried in the field behind our farmhouse . . . priceless.

I'm like a walking MasterCard commercial from the 1990s. Seriously. But it's just how I see life and the value of things, especially our home. Appreciation doesn't depreciate. It just doesn't. I could give you a thousand more examples of intangible value that our farm has, but I need only to think of two: to have been given the gift of a place where we could bring one life forth and lay another one to rest on our property are alone beyond priceless to me.

If you love where you live . . . if you truly decide to love where you live and dig in and live there . . . truly live there, it doesn't matter whether you got ripped off or stole it when you bought it; the value of your home will be much more than a professional home estimate could ever be.

Yes, I know there might come a time when we'll have to sell this place (God forbid), and then those things will matter, but, honestly, I don't think they're gonna matter then either. If I spent a million dollars on our place and in the end it sells for one hundred grand, I would think, *Hmmm . . . it was worth a whole lot more than that to me.* But I guess not to other folks. And it would be what it will be. And life will go on.

I try to remember each day that it could burn to the ground, or a big gust of circling wind could knock it off its stone foundation and level it. And all our stuff and history would be scattered all over the mud-soaked ashes. That would suck. Big-time. But it is far, far from the end of the world.

If I keep in mind that it can happen at any time and remind myself that it's all just a gift, then I won't be too shocked if it were to come to pass. And we would pick up whatever is left and move on. And, in time, I believe we'd find another house that we would start investing our precious time and money in and start building another home that probably won't look good on paper. But it'll be a hell of a place to come have dinner.

Location, Location, Location

It doesn't matter where you are . . . just
as long as you're actually there.

Our story could've started anywhere . . . maybe in one of the other houses I looked at first, before buying the farmhouse we live in, or in a condo or townhouse in another town or state. Looking back, I don't think the location we chose made the story what it has become. I think it has more to do with actually deciding that where we were is where we were supposed to be. And believing it.

Over the years in our travels, Joey and I have seen other places where we could imagine living . . . a ranch in Montana or Jackson Hole, Wyoming . . . a small town in New England . . . or a little beach village on the coast of Italy. And for a few minutes or a few days, our minds would run away with us. We'd let our imaginations take hold and begin to wonder about living a better life than the one we had. And it was always fun to think about those things, but we knew it was just dreaming. We weren't going to give up what we have for something better. Because we knew the truth of it. It wouldn't be better. It would be different but not better.

When you haven't been to the beach in a long time, your first glimpse and your first stroll in the sand with the waves crashing in is intoxicating. The same way with the mountains. The air just smells different, and the sound of the wind in the trees is magical. Not to mention the picturesque valleys and views from a cabin porch, a mile or so in the sky.

And it's not hard to picture a more romantic, sweeter life in one of those places. But there's always a price to pay . . . a cost that has nothing to do with the selling price of our home and the buying of another. We knew that we would lose something very special to gain something else. The old adage is true, you know . . . you can't have it all. And in the same way, you can't be in more than one place at any given time.

So we have tried to do our best to bloom where we are planted. To be present in the place we are.

My kids used to tell me that I'm not here. I'd say, "Of course I am . . . I'm right here." But that's not what they meant. Yes, I was there physically, but I was also other places. Multitasking in my head. Badly.

If I'm not careful, I will be somewhere and not be there at exactly the same time. I will miss this moment, thinking about another. My mind will be working overtime, even though my body is standing or sitting still. And I'll get this glazed-over look that they recognize right away where I see their mouths moving, but I'm not hearing a word they're saying.

It's not that I didn't care what they were saying because I did. It's just that I wasn't great at being present. The lights are on, so to speak . . . but I'm not home. I'm writing a song or editing a film or thinking about something I should have done or said earlier that day. My girls never got mad. They just shut down little by little. They waited me out. They knew sooner or later I would realize that I'm the one who's missing out on some of the best parts of life and in time would figure it out. And I have. I believe I have.

It doesn't come naturally to me. I have to work at it. To focus on today and let yesterday and tomorrow be. But it's so, so worth it.

All we have is today. Actually, we don't even have that. We have right now. This very moment we're in. And that is enough.

Three Chords and the Truth

Country music is life.

I moved to Nashville in 1995 and became a full-time songwriter not long after. Though for a time, when I was younger, I had visions of being on stage and singing, I soon learned it was in the crafting and combining of lyrics and music where my real gift lay. And so that's what I did. From '95 until '08, when God would magically shine a spotlight on my beautiful bride and I happened to be standing next to her when it happened and somehow ended up in the spotlight too.

But for all the years before that, it was just me and a guitar and a pen, and it was amazing. Making something out of nothing. Including myself.

The songs that I wrote would carry me and my two daughters from barely scraping by to a home and a life that anyone would be proud of. From having nothing to having more than enough. From a lifetime mindset of scarcity to the belief in abundance and seeing the power of generosity.

And the songs themselves would travel from scribbles on blank sheets of paper in empty rooms to arena-sized stadiums with artists like Blake Shelton and Kenny Chesney performing them while throngs of people sang along with every word.

I have always loved writing songs. Seeing the blank page start to fill with words and those words start to reveal a character and the character starts to tell a story.

Many songs end the same way . . . with smeared words and lines near the bottom of the page that are hard to read because my tears had started falling as I came to understand what the song was about and what the character's story was teaching me. And something inside me knew that if a song moved me, there was a good chance it would move others.

My first publishing deal was with the legendary Harlan Howard. I had stalked my way into a meeting with him (if you can call drinking beer on a stool next to him a meeting) and left with an opportunity to write for one of the greats. For five years he and his wife, Melanie, mentored me and helped me understand what it was to be a great songwriter. Harlan is well known for saying that country music is "three chords and the truth." That as a genre, it is simple. And he's right, in my opinion.

What makes country music country music, I believe, is the honesty. The truth-telling, even when it hurts. And most of the time in country songs, it hurts like hell. I was drawn to the country genre's unique form of storytelling at an early age, and I'm still awed by the lyrics of a great country song. When Vern Gosdin sang about not knowing lonely until it's chiseled in stone . . . or when Merle Haggard sang about his mother's hungry eyes, they were speaking into my soul. Talking about my life. My family. My heart.

And so I took to songwriting with all I had. Pouring my guts into it. My heart and my soul.

I remember one time being in Harlan's office and playing a song for him. Back then we recorded our songs on cassette tapes, and that's what I handed Harlan that morning and what he put in his tape deck and pushed play. As he sat and listened, I was parked on the leather couch nearby. Songwriting had been very good to Harlan in the last forty years, and his office showed it. Immaculately built and decorated. It was an honor just to be sitting there beside him, let alone playing songs for him.

The song was called "That's Good Enough for Me." About a farmer who had never been outside the small rural county he lived in. He'd never seen the ocean or had a midnight rendezvous with a lover, but he'd watched the flowers grow in his garden, and he'd known what it feels like to love and be true to one woman, and that was good enough for him.

Harlan listened to the whole song with his eyes closed. When it ended, he pushed stop, but he didn't say, "I like it," or "I don't like it." Instead, he said, "I love this guy." Like the character in the song was a real person. "I'm not him," Harlan continued, "but I wish I was." And Harlan went on to talk about the man in the song and his character and how a part of him wishes he were more like this farmer.

That conversation changed my songwriting forever. Honestly, I don't remember if he said whether he liked the song or not. All I remember is that he treated the character in the song and the story as if he was a real man . . . he hurt and felt for him as if he was a real-life human being here on earth with us. And that in turn gave me license to do the same thing.

Because of Harlan, the characters in my songs aren't just imaginary people who are one-dimensional to me. Instead, they are just like anyone else I meet on this journey through life that I'm on. They are people who have something to say, something to show you, and something to pass on to us. And I treat them as if they are real. Because, in a sense, they are.

If I write or hear a song about a man who has come to realize that he's learned how to love his wife from the people he has dated or loved in his past . . . it is not much different than if I had learned the same thing from my brother or my buddy at Muletown Coffee or my grandfather. Either way, I have observed or listened to someone who has shared something important with me. Something I need to know to help me on my journey. And afterward, in both cases, I have only the memory of the experience to guide me . . . whether that's from an interaction with a real-life person or with a make-believe character in a song.

Movies are the same way. I can't begin to tell you how much Forrest Gump has impacted my life and my desire to live simpler, with more innocence and love. It doesn't matter that he is a fictional character from a book and movie. It only matters that I saw him and I heard him do things that have inspired me.

I believe that it's the same way, actually, with Jesus. None of us have met Him. Only through the books in the New Testament and the story of His life and words. And from that, we are continually learning how to become better men and women and followers of Him.

"You're a soul man, Rory," Harlan went on to say that day, with a smile on his face and a burning cigarette in his hand. I wasn't sure how to respond . . . part of me wondering if Harlan's seventy-plus years were catching up with him. I guess he could see my wheels spinning and the confusion in my mind. "What I mean is that you write from your soul, son."

Then he took another drag from his cigarette and went on to tell me the story about when he wrote "I Fall to Pieces" for Patsy Cline. I had heard it before. A dozen times probably, but I acted as if I was hearing it for the first. And that story turned into a Buck Owens story, then one about listening to his hero Ernest Tubb play the Opry on the radio when he was a boy growing up somewhere outside of Detroit.

I loved Harlan's stories, and I so wish he were still around so he could tell them to me a dozen times more. Or so my kids could gather at his feet and listen the way I got to so many times. Harlan passed away in 2002, but he left behind thousands of songs filled with characters who have gone on to teach countless people about life.

Each one of them nothing more than . . . three chords and the truth.

I Hold the Pen

. . . but God writes the song.

It's true. At least when the song is great—when it's special . . . it's all Him. I'm just holding the pen. God's doing the heavy lifting.

A year or so after moving to Nashville, I had a songwriting appointment.

I opened my spiral notebook and found a pencil as Austin Cunningham, the writer I was meeting with, reached into his bag and pulled out a beautiful leather-bound journal that seemed to magically open to the next empty page he was looking for. I pretended not to be paying any attention to it, but I watched as he wrote what I thought was going to be his name on the top right side of the page and then mine as the cowriter he was working with (pretty standard practice for writers), but that wasn't what he wrote. Instead, the first name he put on the page was "God." Then below that was his name. Then mine.

Hmmm . . . , I thought. *Wonder why he's doing that?* We spent the day working on a song together and had a wonderful time. I can't remember what we wrote, but I do remember feeling that he was an anointed writer and man. Filled with the Spirit in a way that I was not. Born and raised Catholic, he was a kind, gentle person with an incredibly strong faith in God that showed in just about everything he did and said.

I wasn't there yet. I was still a few years away. But I was searching. Even if it was only in my time frame.

The next writing appointment I had, I opened my spiral notebook the same way I always had, but this time . . . the first name and thing I wrote on the page was "Jesus." I figured if Austin had God, then maybe Jesus was available for the claiming. And so from that moment on, until pretty much now, I had a cowriter that I brought to every writing appointment I've ever had. Whether my other cowriter knew it or not.

Through the years Austin and I have become good friends. Joey and I recorded his song "Made to Last" on one of our albums a few years ago. But I don't believe I've ever asked him about his notebook or *God* being in the top right-hand corner of the page. And in the same way no one has really ever asked me why Jesus is my cowriter. Actually, my daughter Heidi saw it on my lyric sheet years ago and asked me about it and has long since been aware that I believe that's where some of the magic comes from. It has made a difference in my songwriting and in my musical career. Mostly because it is there as a reminder of where the songs come from. Where whatever gift I have has come from and where all the credit for anything I am part of making should go.

To Him. The One who truly writes the songs.

I have carried that concept on to pretty much every kind of story-telling that I do, whether it's writing a book, like this one or my first one, *This Life I Live*, or a film we're making or a blog post I'm writing. I am a part of the creative process, and I've done my homework. I know the craft of storytelling well. But He is the great storyteller, and all the great ideas and lines come from Him. Anything mediocre or so-so is definitely from me.

The magic isn't just in writing the words *God* or *Jesus*, though, it's in believing that with His help anything is possible. That He can take average talent like ours and turn it into a piece of art that wins Grammy Awards and impacts millions of lives. He can do anything. It doesn't mean that He will, but He could . . . and the belief and the hope in Him is where the magic lies.

Though I have recently started trying to do some songwriting again, I'm a long way from being back in full swing. It's been a few years for me since I've done any songwriting or even wanted to, and I'm just taking baby steps so far. But even that is exciting. Because I know what can come from a blank page. A blank page that is filled with His Spirit.

Video Rewind

Watching my kids when they were kids.

Heidi and Hopie were about six and eight years old, and we were living in an apartment complex on the west side of Nashville. It was before my songwriting career had cranked up, and I was making a living by traveling back and forth to Texas playing shows. A neighbor and friend named Buffy Lawson offered to watch the kids one weekend while I had to be gone. But she did much, much more than just babysit my girls. She turned that weekend into a treasure.

Buffy was a wonderful singer who had moved to Nashville in search of fame and fortune like a thousand other people in the early to mid '90s, including me. She and I had written a few songs together, and she had become a sweet friend to me and to my girls. So her offer to watch them wasn't just a blessing to me, it was exciting for the kids. She was fun and had lived in Las Vegas at one time and had a closetful of show clothes. Frilly things the kids could play dress-up in. I knew they were in good hands, so that Friday morning, I kissed them goodbye and headed to the airport.

The weekend was pretty uneventful for me. I played an early show at Risky's BBQ in Sundance Square in downtown Fort Worth on Friday evening and then a later show at the Red Goose—a historical old shoe store that had been converted into a restaurant and honky-tonk. I played another show there on Saturday night and the next morning caught the JetBlue flight home to Nashville.

When I got to Buffy's apartment, the kids were grinning ear to ear. Sitting on the couch with their stuff in grocery bags, so excited to see me. But before we left, Buffy said they had something to show me.

Buffy walked over to the TV and popped a VHS tape into the player, and the kids hopped on my lap as she pushed play. And for the next fifteen minutes, my little ones came alive on the big screen. While songs from the soundtrack of *The Lion King* played, Hopie and Heidi paraded in and out of Buffy's living room in different dresses and hats, all of them way too big for their little bodies. Dancing and sashaying to the music and laughing and giggling . . . Heidi always on the beat and Hopie doing exactly what her big sister was doing, only a second or two behind her. It was precious. And just when I thought it couldn't be any cuter, the music and dancing ended and the girls came on screen and one by one said, "Dad, I just wanted to tell you I love you so much and am so thankful for you. You're the best dad a kid could ever have!"

I melted.

Actually, that's what Heidi said. When Hopie's time on camera came, through her toothless grin, she said, "Dad . . . I just want to thank you for whatever it is that you did for me," along with a bunch of other things that had not much to do with me at all. And then I hear Buffy and Heidi say, "Cut," then tell her to thank me for whatever it is that she wants to thank me for . . . and, again, she says the same thing. It was so darn cute.

Fast-forward twenty-five years. And if I thought it was cute then, it's magical now. I didn't grow up in a world of video cameras, so there's nothing of me on video as a child. And, unfortunately, there's not much of my girls on video either. Not because there couldn't have been but because I just didn't think to buy a camera and capture those moments. I could have, but I just didn't.

But, thankfully, Buffy did. Hopie gets nervous whenever we pull out the VHS tape with faded "B-H-H" written in Sharpie on it. She's embarrassed by what she said and how she said it. Her little six-year-old speech impediment turning all the *r*'s into *w*'s. But I don't think she realizes yet how special it is. And how special she is. How very special both she and Heidi are.

I still cross paths with Buffy every now and then in Nashville and am always quick to hug her and thank her again and again for the gift she gave us. She didn't have to do that, but she did. She turned a weekend of watching my little girls into a lifetime of watching "my little girls."

Daddy, What If?

Like father . . . like daughters.

Heidi and Hopie grew up around music.

It was either being played at our house or in the car on a cassette tape or the radio, or we were somewhere watching or listening to people play. Even more so, they grew up listening to their father play music. From time to time they were even part of it.

When we lived in Texas, I played a thousand shows for dozens of people. At least that's how it felt. Sometimes there would be almost no one in the room, and sometimes there would be a decent number of folks listening or dancing. It wasn't something I enjoyed doing at the time, but I realized later how important it was. For those songs to get inside of me and affect the songwriter I would become. But those songs were also getting inside the girls. They are the soundtrack to their lives or at least a big chunk of their early lives.

Neither Heidi nor Hopie listen to much country music on the radio today. They are not necessarily big fans of it. But both of them know just about everything about the songs and artists and country music from the 1990s.

When we moved to Nashville, I played songwriters' nights all around town. At the Bluebird Cafe, the Boardwalk, Broken Spoke, and a dozen other places. A lot of the time there weren't many more people in those rooms either. But the people who were in the room changed everything. Many of them became close friends and cowriters; some of them I've even written hit songs with through the years. A handful became famous singers themselves.

And somewhere in the back of the room, or next to me inside a guitar case, would be Hopie sleeping. She was still small enough to fit inside, and she could drift off to sleep when she got tired. Heidi was drinking a Cherry Coke, soaking up every word and every line. She loved the music almost as much as I did. She does still in a lot of ways.

But in the years before we moved to Nashville, the girls not only saw me on stage playing; from time to time they joined me. Especially Heidi. There were a few songs we would sing together, like "Don't Cry Joni" by Conway Twitty and his daughter, and "Pretty Woman" (Hopie loved that one), but the one we loved to sing the most was "Daddy What If" by Bobby Bare and his son Bobby Bare Jr. Growing up as a little boy, I had heard that song on the radio and had sung it with my father, or at least tried, while sitting in the car next to him. It isn't a song that my dad ever learned how to play, but I think he liked it, and I loved it. Even more so, I loved the idea of it.

So when I had children of my own, they would sing it with me. On the wall in my office is a framed piece of paper with the lyrics for the song. I typed it out when Heidi was very small and with a crayon drew pictures of important lines . . . a "sun" for when she would sing about the sun shining, a "rain cloud" for when she would sing about the rain, and a "boat" for when she would sing about a boat. And so, before she could read, she learned to sing. She learned to sing with her father. And it wasn't just cute . . . it was precious. And on top of that, it was a money maker.

The most I would make in one evening playing for four hours was a hundred dollars. But I also got tips, and when Heidi and I would sing the song, even when she was only six or seven, the money would start rolling in. It wasn't unusual for us to get three or four twenty-dollar bills in the tip jar after singing it. That made a big difference in our life.

But the truth is, I didn't have Heidi sing it because I wanted to make money; it was because I loved it so much. I loved what it said, and I loved singing with her and with Hopie. I'm sure Heidi still knows every single word even though she's thirty-one years old now. And she remembers those times on stage with me and how people responded to her singing with me. I wish I had a video of those moments . . . just one of them.

Something tells me that when little Indiana gets older, she, too, will be singing about the "sunshine" and the "rain" falling, but for her, it will probably be called "Papa What If." And though there may not be tip jars, there will be people with their own "rain" falling from their eyes. Especially mine.

Monday, Monday

The start of a new week. A new everything.

I love Mondays. Most people dread them. I'm always excited to see them come. It can be a Tuesday morning, and I'm already thinking about the coming Monday. It's weird.

But it's because Monday is much more than just the start of another week for me. Mondays are the start of everything. They are the New Year's Day of the seven-day week. When anything is possible. But you have to start then. You can't start on a Wednesday or a Friday or even a Sunday. It has to be Monday. It's the rule.

But who made that rule? Where in the world did I get that idea and why has it stuck with me for so long? Monday is actually just another day. Maybe even a crappier one than many of the other days in the week. So why is it that I think it's so special? Not sure. It just is.

My kids are the same way, unfortunately. If you ever hear Heidi talk about starting a new diet or when she's gonna make a change in her life . . . it's gonna be on a Monday. Hopie is the same way, I think. Yep, they got it from me. And I got it from . . . well, I'm not sure where I got it from. It's just one of those weird things that's inside my head. Like how the number eight is better than other numbers. Or how white is my favorite color (even though people keep trying to tell me that white is not actually a color). Mondays are the day of fresh starts.

I got a hunch that it's a bunch of bullarkey. That it, of course, is just all in my head (and maybe a few million other people's heads in the world), and any day of the week is, actually, just as good for changing. That what I'm really after is "a day"—a specified time to make a change. And not only to make it but believe it can happen, and, for some reason, I think Monday's got magic in it. And because I think that . . . it has some. Big-time.

I've changed lots of things on Mondays. Some have been small, like starting a workout program. And some tougher, like giving up coffee or alcohol. And, for some reason, if I start on a Monday . . . there's about a gazillion times better chance that I'm gonna follow through. It's ridiculous, I know. But the good kind of ridiculous. The kind that I think maybe I specialize in.

Right now, it's Wednesday in the late afternoon, and I've been trying to figure out a clear vision for a new project I've been working on for a couple of weeks. And though I've spent a good bit of time thinking 'bout it today and even making a few notes on my laptop . . . something inside is nudging me. Saying . . . *You know better than this. You're not going to find it this week. Gonna have to wait till Monday.*

Powerful little bugger, isn't it? Somehow invades every part of my creativity and rains a lot of doubt on my parade. At least it does for six days a week, but come Monday, though, the confidence comes pouring out. And it works. Most of the time anyway. It's crazy, I know. But the facts are the facts.

Recently, though, Mondays are starting to have their own little Monday requirements. It seems that starting something on a Monday is no longer good enough. Now, if I haven't started it by about 7 a.m. on Monday morning, the day's shot . . . and, subsequently, the whole week is shot with it. A couple of weeks ago I was gonna start a new routine for working out, and the plan was to start this past Monday. Well, when I got up on Monday morning, I made coffee and started folding laundry before the baby woke up and suddenly realized that it was a Monday. I looked at the clock and thought, *Dang it.* I blew it. It was almost 7 a.m. and too late on a Monday to start.

And so it, too, will have to wait for next week. For Monday's Monday. I better set a reminder on my phone so I don't forget.

Brilliant Limitations

It's our limitations that create our style.

—Chuck Berry

I am only a mediocre guitar player, and that is part of what makes me so good at what I do.

When one area is weak, another area shines through. If I were an incredible player, my words would be less important. I think it is because of the weakness of some of my musical abilities that my lyrical abilities stand out. I am thankful for that.

I've tried many times to learn to be a better guitar player. I bought some tutorial videos and even took a couple of lessons, but it didn't help. My heart wasn't in it.

I have also tried to be more proficient at other instruments, with the hope that while I may have been given "okay" guitar prowess, I could possibly be a prodigy on something else. Maybe I just hadn't discovered it.

And so for one birthday, Joey gave me an upright bass. I thought that for sure I'd be a genius on it in time. Heck, it only had four strings and you only had to hit one at a time. How hard could that be? Turns out that the greats on bass—studio players like Kevin Grantt—have spent a lifetime working on developing their gift. It wasn't an overnight thing.

And so, though I could play along with some songs and was fairly good at it, I put it down and picked my guitar back up.

A year or so later Joey got me a mandolin. *This one should be super easy. It's teeny weeny. Anyone could learn to master this,* I thought. Maybe my fingers were too big, probably just my expectations. But either way I wasn't very good. I gave that mandolin to our fiddle player. I knew he would play it, and he does. I see it on TV, in shows he's playing from time to time.

I've gone on to have visions of grandeur about playing banjo (there's one sitting right here by my desk), piano, and a few other things on my list of things I can't play. But the intention is always there. The hope. In time those things get put into check by the truth. I'm a word guy.

There was probably a much simpler (and cheaper) solution to all of this than spending weeks and months and years on all these different instruments. I could've probably saved myself a ton of time just by asking, "What brings me to tears . . . what truly moves me and makes me cry . . . ?" That's easy. Songs. Lyrics. Stories.

And so that's where I try to spend my time. Writing stories. Living stories. Capturing them and sharing them with others.

It is one of the things I love about filmmaking . . . the story aspect of it. I love that I can start with nothing . . . and create something special. Something that moves me deeply and makes me cry or laugh and both at the same time. Whether it's a blog video or music project or TV show or even a film. It is storytelling.

And, for some reason, the visual part of it is more powerful than even music. To me it is. Especially when video is combined with music. I can listen to a song and be touched. Moved. But if I add the right images in the right places and listen again while I watch . . . what moved me before will kill me now. I will be in a puddle of tears on the floor.

I read somewhere that to be great at something, you need to put in at least ten thousand hours of practice. Let's see, if I looked at that like a job . . . I'd have to spend forty hours a week for almost five straight years of my life, working five days a week, eight hours a day, to learn to be great at something. That is a ton of time.

And time is something I don't have an unlimited amount of. So, instead, I have realized there will be lots and lots of things I'm not going to be great at. Things I might enjoy or even think are worthwhile . . . but I'll never master them. And that's okay with me.

I have learned to be perfectly happy with playing my guitar the way I play it. And with sitting down at the piano in the living room just messing around. Finding sounds and chords I like and enjoying it for what it is. Music. My music. Not the best. Not the worst. But it's mine.

And Indiana likes to hear me play, just like her mama did before her. And that's good enough for me.

The Bus Stops Here

My education of the education system.

I went to school wherever the big yellow bus that picked me up in front of the house we lived in took me.

It was as simple as that. My mother didn't stress out about whether or not my brothers and sisters and I were getting a good education in the schools we were in; it was just what it was. We got whatever we got. And, somehow, it worked out fine.

And so when I grew up and had kids, I thought the same logic would hold true for mine, but it didn't. Not by a long shot.

When Heidi and Hopie became school age, I did what my mother did . . . let my kids go to school wherever the bus that stopped in front of our apartment or house took them . . . but the schools they went to failed them. Even more than that, I failed my older daughters when it came to their education.

By the time Heidi was in fifth grade and Hopie in third, it was clear that the plan I had wasn't working for them. For us. Heidi was being bused to an inner-city school in Nashville even though we lived in the suburbs (an effort by the city to try to make amends for different incomes, backgrounds, etc. that didn't really work) . . . and she suffered on account of it. But it was Hopie who suffered the most. Her math and reading skills developed slower than Heidi's did and slower than those of some of the other children her age. So she fell behind early on. When she was in third grade, I was in a meeting with her teachers, and the principal of the school told me that whatever hopes I had for Hopie having a higher education . . . I needed to rethink them. They made that decision that early and didn't really even give her a chance.

I refused to listen to them, but, subconsciously, in the back of my mind, I think I let them tell me how it was going to be. And Hopie fell further and further behind. Hopie was a ninth-grader and in a free fall by the time Joey and I were married, and I finally became aware that there are other education options and I needed to look at them. But by then it was too late. Other schools would've gladly taken my money and tried to help Hopie, but what she needed was something much different, much sooner.

Looking back, I don't think it was so much that Hopie needed the right school to go to as much as she needed someone who could say that this push to make everyone learn the same things the same way is a bunch of bunk. And the constant message to kids that getting into and going to college is the most important thing. I believe that reading and writing and arithmetic are fine, but a child's character and life skills and compassion and heart are even more important than those things. Way, way more important than whether they go to college or get a degree. And Hopie's scores in those areas from day one of school were off the charts.

But I let the school system fool me into thinking that Hopie was failing. That she wasn't as good as the other kids. Even more so, I let Hopie believe that she wasn't. She is twenty-nine years old now, and she believes it still. And it breaks my heart. Even as I write these words, I know her . . . and I know she is worried that I will write something that makes her look bad or gives the impression that she wasn't as smart as other children were or as other women her age are now. But I am telling you, Hopie is brilliant, and she always has been.

Me, on the other hand, as Hopie was growing up . . . I needed some work. I was nowhere near the kind of father I should've been. The father that she and her big sister, Heidi, needed and deserved me to be.

A few years after Joey and I got married, I started doing some research, looking into homeschool and alternative education solutions in other parts of the country and the world, and realized that there are other great options available out there if you just seek them out. In Hopie's last couple of years of school, I tried to assert myself and homeschool her, but I wasn't prepared to do what I needed to do. To be who I needed to be as her father. I was still trying to do everything else and be everything else at the same time, and she got what was left over. She got my love but not my full attention.

I wish I could go back in time and redo so many things about the kids' school years and put their hearts and their character development first, above their grades at school and test scores. That is probably why I have such an interest in Indiana's future. In her education. And why I am trying to make some big decisions if that's what it takes to give her what she needs to learn and be her best.

In some ways, Indiana's education is easier, I think. Mostly because when people look at her, they expect her to be slower . . . to have lower grades and not be able to learn things as fast or in the same way as other kids. Hopie, on the other hand, didn't have that luxury. She looked the same as every other kid. Maybe prettier or taller but the same on the outside. So they expected her to think and process and be the same on the inside too. And that's a shame, in my opinion.

Mayberry

Trying to live in black and white.

Mount Pleasant is a little town about thirty minutes from our farm. It has a simple but charming downtown area with historic old buildings lining the street, and the first time I drove into it, there was a 1950s diner on the corner. I fell in love with it immediately.

A few months later I helped my sister open a small knickknack shop called Marcy's Uniques & Antiques and was spending so much time there that I decided to open my own place. I rented a restored empty building where an old hardware store had been and set up a studio. Only I didn't sell or show anything, I just worked there by myself. Writing songs and dreaming.

A lot of amazing things happened during the time I was in that little town. But the biggest one was meeting my wife, Joey. She happened to come to a songwriters' night that I started in the hall above the '50s diner, and that's where we met. Six months later that hall was also where we had our wedding reception. Just down the street is the church where we got married, and across from that is where I tore down an old house to try to reclaim an almost two-hundred-year-old log cabin that was beneath it.

For some reason, actually lots of them, that little town resonated with me. It was like a place from my past. Or, more likely, a place that I wished was from my past. I had given my heart and life to God a year or two before, and He had been working on my character, leading me to be more than I was. To need less than I had.

And so I found myself setting up shop in that songwriting studio across from my sister and just down from the diner. It was Mayberry. Or at least I thought it was or could be. My girls were starting their seventh- and ninth-grade school years, and the schools that they'd been in weren't working for them. They needed and deserved something better. And so I pulled them out of those schools and enrolled them in the ones in the small town. The kids rode the half hour or so to work with me in the morning, and I'd drop them off at school and park my truck a few blocks away in the square at my office. When school was over, they could walk to my office. I had installed a vintage Coke machine in my office, and it was filled with ice-cold soda bottles that they could enjoy after school.

It was heavenly. Actually, mostly the idea of it was heavenly. If you know me, you know that I see things a little differently than most people do. I somehow see the best side of things, the kindest, gentlest parts. And the parts that other people see first, the parts that keep them from jumping in with both feet . . . I somehow don't even notice.

And for a while in that little town, it worked. It was sweet. I loved the people who worked in the other shops and the sense of community that had come with being there. Marcy and I would have coffee and a honey bun together at the diner every morning—something that we did in our childhood with our father . . . a memory recreated that you could live every day. And it was so neat. And I would visit with the local men who met for coffee, and they welcomed me in . . . the retired banker, the judge, the man who oversaw the electric company. And I'd get my hair cut at Speedy's barbershop. It truly felt like a moment from another time.

Unfortunately, it was a moment from another time, and the truth of the era we were living in began to show up in a big way. First off, one morning I stopped in for coffee, and there was no one in the cafe, so I walked into the back room, and everyone was glued around a TV. Stunned. A plane had crashed into one of the Twin Towers in NYC. None of us could believe it. And as I stood there watching, another plane hit the other tower.

It was a wake-up call to the world and also to my little world. Things were not as rosy as they seemed.

A few blocks away both my girls started struggling with their new schools. The town had a brand-new middle school with a beautiful new arts department and stage, but Hopie was lost and way behind and felt even more alone than ever. Heidi was fitting in with the small-town kids in the high school, but it wasn't a good thing. The school was drug-ridden, and a large number of the girls dropped out of school early, pregnant.

Heidi joined the girls' volleyball team, and the school couldn't afford to hire a coach, so they had a science teacher, who had no idea how to play volleyball, take over the job. I offered to come help. To coach for free. I played tons of volleyball in the service (a couple years of tournament play and coached a women's team in Hawaii). It was a great idea, but a number of girls were unruly and foul-mouthed, and it made me want to find a way to be an even better coach and mentor to them and put in place a rule about no foul language. One of the parents complained, and the school board decided to have the teacher, who had never seen a volleyball, coach them instead. A short time later Heidi quit the team and never went back to volleyball.

My sister's shop had to close down because there were no customers. I mean none. She might sell two dollars' worth of stuff in a day or sometimes a week. The problem was that no one was coming to the square. Coming to town at all. The locals all shopped at the big-box retailers in Columbia, where you could get things cheaper and had more choices, and the tourists had no idea where this town was. And I began to see all the infighting among the shop owners. Though there were a number of people who believed in the town and saw the potential, they were overwhelmed by the ones who had been there their whole lives and accepted the status quo.

And I began to realize that you can't will a town to life, no matter how much you try.

When Joey and I got married, she encouraged me to rethink what I was doing. She knew what I was trying to do there in that little town with my work and my girls—the life I was trying to live—but she also knew that it wasn't realistic and where we were wasn't the best thing for the kids or for me.

So we let the lease on the hardware store run out and sold the log cabin that we worked on and moved back home to the farm. We had never really left the farm, not really. For that year or so, we had been trying to juggle two lives and had put off living one there at the farm, in search of a better one somewhere else. Joey knew that was never gonna work and let me know that we needed to invest our time and money and lives in only one of them. And for her, there was only one real choice. Only one life that held a future for us, and that was at our farm.

And so I pulled the kids out of school again and moved our lives back to the farm. Heidi would end up in a private Christian school for her last three years and Hopie, too, for a while then homeschool. But, in the end, I think I hurt them more than helped them by pulling up stakes and moving to Mayberry.

The idea was solid, I think. A good one. But, in the end, the location was wrong. I have come to realize that Mayberry can still be . . . it just has to be wherever you are. You make Mayberry. We all do if we want it. And so it turns out it is right here. In our little community where my wife and sister's restaurant, Marcy Jo's, is and where our neighbors and we live. Hardison Mill. Pottsville. It is our Mayberry . . . a magical place that is straight out of another time. A TV show come to life. But it's not perfect. It's far from that. Nothing ever will be, and that's okay. It just has to be perfect for us. And it is.

I made the trip back to Mount Pleasant this past June on Joey's and my fifteenth anniversary. My cousin Aaron and I had dinner in the place where that diner used to be, and we walked the streets, and I told him stories from when we had tried to build a life there. And it was neat. Sadly, most of the stores and streets are still empty, and buildings are in worse shape than before. The hardware store where I had put my studio looks like it did when I walked away from it, only worse.

But there is growth in this area. Columbia, the town closest to where we live, is becoming more popular, and people are buying properties right and left and moving here from all over. The downtown square has been immaculately restored, and all the businesses are thriving. My guess is that Mount Pleasant will be next. In the next ten years or so, it will probably have its day again, and the streets will be filled and stores bustling with activity. And it will be what I hoped it was and more for someone else. For lots of people . . . looking for their own Mayberry.

Some Barn

Build it . . . and they will come.

I wanted a place to tinker on old cars. A man cave of sorts where I could turn rusty bolts with wrenches and get away from the hustle and grind of the music business. Joey and I had talked about building a new barn for a couple years, but it just didn't make any sense at the time, and, besides, there was no real way to pay for it. But in 2004, a song about being on some beach somewhere changed that.

Paul Overstreet and I had met at a Starbucks near his farm in west Nashville one morning and were sitting drinking coffee and talking about song ideas we might write that day. One of us said "some beach" in a way that sounded like the *ea* in *beach* had a bit more of an *i* sound to it. And as men, who are just overgrown little boys, will do, we started giggling and singing more lines. Pretty soon we were sitting in Paul's boat on Percy Priest Lake with a couple guitars in our hands, trying to get into character for this song we were writing about a beach.

I remember the sun starting to set on the water and my flip phone ringing with "JOEY" in big letters on the screen and me pretending that I didn't see it. More than once. It's not that I didn't want to talk to her, it's just that we were on a roll and were getting dangerously close to finishing the song. By the time I got in my truck and called Joey back, saying something about "bad reception" and "lost track of time," the song was complete. Even more than that, it sounded like a hit. And before long, it was.

Most songs take years to find their way to an artist who's willing to listen to them, let alone go into a studio and record them, but this one moved pretty quickly from Starbucks to stage. In no more than a couple months, it was on the radio and burning up the charts. It wouldn't stop climbing until it reached number one (the third song I'd had reach the top spot on *Billboard*), and it stayed there for a couple of weeks.

I knew there'd be some extra zeroes on some checks in the mailbox before long, so I brought up the barn to Joey again. "You deserve it," she said, and that was it. In no time a forty-by-seventy-foot man cave was erected just across our driveway. With three bay doors and a workshop, it was just what I had always wanted and more. We called it "Some Barn" because it was built with the money from "Some Beach." And to say that it's been *some barn* is a huge understatement.

For a couple years it was just that . . . a barn. A spot where I could tinker on old cars I'd bought for three hundred bucks or a wooden boat a neighbor said I could have if I would just haul it out of their barn. And it was fun. For a while. Life got busy, and all my best intentions never really came to be. The cars never ran, and the boat didn't float. The junk was still just junk, only there was now more of it.

Until one day we needed a place to film a Christmas TV special. And to rent a soundstage in Nashville would've cost a small fortune. So my buddies and I just pushed all that junk into the far sides of the barn and started filming. It was rinky-dink with a homemade backdrop and borrowed lights, but it was honest, and, in the end, it made all the difference. That TV special we made soon became a weekly television show, then more TV specials, and then dozens of live concerts. And that barn is where it all happened.

The big red barn on our property cost around sixty thousand to build, and it's made ten or twenty times that amount back for us. Even more than that, it completely changed the game for us. We went from being a small part of the huge music industry to creating our own unique cottage industry. A place where we could grow a career and a life at the same time.

And it isn't just that barn. We kinda did the same thing with the other buildings on the property too. The brick dairy barn where the Blalocks used to milk cows is a full 7.1 surround-sound editing and mixing studio and houses tons of film and camera gear that we use to make the things we make. Before that, it was my songwriting studio and before that, a makeshift gym to work out in.

The small tool barn by the house is now half garden shed and half henhouse. One side filled with white and buff-rock hens and a Rhode Island red rooster that come in and out of a door that automatically opens and closes with the rising and falling of the sun, and the other half full of hoes and hand spades, baskets and ball jars. All part of Joey's master plan to keep our lives and bodies as healthy as the soil she planted in.

Just like all the other buildings and spots here on the farm. When we moved in, it was all random. Empty barns and buildings that came with the old farmhouse that we had our hearts set on buying. When I think about how much has happened in those buildings, and because of those buildings, it's easy to see that they all are a part of a greater master plan that none of us could see. Only God knew what we were building here. Just as He is the only One who knows where it will lead us in the future.

Heart Break

Sometimes our broken hearts just need a break.

It was spring of 2011. Joey and I had been on the road for the past couple of years, doing multiple radio tours—trying to get radio stations to play our songs but not getting anywhere. In the country music industry, there's really only one way to move the needle, and that's by having your songs play on the radio. That's how people get to hear your music and, ultimately, how they buy albums and what motivates them to come see you in concert. Otherwise, they have no real way to discover you or your music. No radio means no career. That might be changing now with the Internet and YouTube and Spotify in the picture, but at least that's the way it used to be.

We were both tired of traveling. Tired of boarding planes that were headed everywhere and not getting anywhere. We missed the farm and our family and friends, and we missed our life. We didn't want just to sing about living a life in the country, we still wanted to live it. And so it all came to a head that April at the Academy of Country Music Awards in Las Vegas. Joey and I were worn out. We had won the Top New Artist award the year before and were nominated for Top Country Duo again, but our hearts weren't in it.

We checked into the MGM Grand, feeling defeated long before they gave the trophy to someone else. But not just defeated over the progress we'd made, deflated about the process of it all in the first place.

For the last few months, maybe even the last year or so, we had both started asking the question, what was the point of all this? What does fame and fortune really bring? There we were in the front four rows of another big award show with fifteen thousand fans in the theater and millions watching at home, honored to be there, but really wondering what it's all about. We had become discouraged. Not just by not having more success but by looking around at people who were having huge success and seeing how empty they were and thinking, there has to be more to it than this . . . realizing that, like all things, the music industry is mostly just a big business, like any other business. And wondering, does this really add up to anything worthwhile? We had come to a place where we couldn't honestly answer yes.

There were so many questions in our minds and in our hearts. What were we even there for? What were we trying to accomplish? Become more famous . . . get more money? We both knew we weren't in it for that. And the sacrifice you had to make didn't add up to what you received in return, even if you reached all your goals and made a lot of money or were successful. It costs too much.

And so as we sat there in the audience, holding hands with big smiles on our faces, listening to them say, "And the nominees are . . ." Our hearts were breaking, and inside we were fighting back tears. We didn't want to be there. We wanted to go home. It was time. Joey looked at me and said, "Are you ready?" and I knew what she was asking.

"I've been ready," I said. "Just waiting for you."

And so when we caught our flight to Nashville the next day, we knew it was a one-way trip. We could feel it in our hearts. We still had a few commitments we'd have to fulfill in the coming months, but, for the most part, we were done. Not necessarily done with the music business but done with doing it the way everyone else does it. Done with trying to fit into a model we never were gonna fit into and done sacrificing everything we loved to make it happen.

Within a few weeks we let our manager go, and not too long after that, we also parted from the record label we were on. Both painful breakups but inevitable. In a lot of ways I think they were as relieved as we were. They all loved us, and we loved them. That wouldn't change, but they didn't know what to do with us, and it wasn't working for any of us. Joey and I felt immediate relief with those changes even though we had no idea where we'd go from there.

There had to be a better way. I just believed that there was. And it was my job to find it.

Farmhouse Christmas

Sometimes people saying no is
God's way of saying yes.

Joey spent the summer in the garden doing what she did best. Being present. Coaxing from the soil bright-red tomatoes and purple-hull peas that she had started as seeds in eggshells that came from our chickens. But she was hurting inside, afraid that it was all over. That our moment in the spotlight was gone.

I remember sitting on the swing outside with her in the evenings and her tears falling and me holding her and telling her it was going to be okay. That we'd find another route to go down. Our own route. I know she had her doubts about whether one was out there or not, but she didn't doubt me. She knew I would find one if one could be found.

But those tears were good tears. Tears of relief in some ways. I had seen a lot more tears in the couple years leading up to this. Tears of frustration and disappointment over what it was, not what we'd accomplished. And so those tears were necessary if we were ever gonna move forward and find our own path.

While Joey was in the garden, I was in the milk house. Not milking cows, of course . . . we had long ago converted it into a little studio/office where I could work and write songs. A place where I could "go to work" and still be close enough for Joey to ring the dinner bell if it was time for me to come in for lunch. I did what I always do. I prayed about the situation we were in, and I thought about it . . . what other options we might have to grow a career. And somewhere in there the thought occurred to me that television is how our career got started in the first place . . . what if it's the path that we're supposed to be taking again now?

It made sense. I remember John Hamlin, one of the producers of the CMT show *Can You Duet?* that we had been on originally, saying to us one evening in the middle of a taping . . . "There's something magical happening here . . . I can't take my eyes off you two." And he and I both laughed and joked that, who knows . . . maybe one day we would have our own variety show. It was inconceivable to me at the time and still pretty much was. But stranger things had happened, and I knew that "doing the impossible" was one of God's favorite tricks.

And so I came up with an idea to film a TV special for the Christmas album that we had recorded earlier that spring. *We'll just make it at home*, I thought. *How hard could it be? We'll call it* A Farmhouse Christmas! We had made lots of music videos at home through the years, surely this couldn't be that different. I also knew that we had a friend named Larry Black who made TV shows himself. We had been guests on some of his shows, and each time the experience left a powerful mark on us. For a few reasons. First off, though it was work . . . it somehow felt like being at home around family. And Larry always started every production with a prayer, either on air or off. Praying for God's blessing upon the work they were doing and the people involved. Not something you'll see at most TV tapings you go to, for sure.

So I told Joey my idea, and she liked it. We had a show that we were booked to play at the Montana Music Ranch in a few weeks, and Larry had a cabin near there in Red Lodge, so I asked if we could come see him while we were out that way. He graciously invited us to stay a few days with him and his wife, Luann, at their cabin.

Their cabin is huge, nestled near the top of a mountain range. I remember sitting on one of the big decks that overlooks a gorgeous valley below and being nervous to ask Larry, but I did it anyway. I told him that we were wanting to make a Christmas TV special that could be aired starting in November. And I asked him if he would help us make it. He just sat and listened while I talked and then very politely said, "No, I won't." I was so disappointed. But then he said, "If you figure out how to make it yourself, I will give you some of our airtime at Thanksgiving and Christmas."

That was all I needed to know. Instead of being heartbroken and realizing that I had no idea how to make a TV special, I took it as an opportunity to learn and said, "You've got a deal."

By early October we were filming the special. We hired some friends we knew who had worked with us on some of the music videos we made, and I moved all the old cars and boat and junk out of the way in the barn, and our handyman, Thomas Travioli, built a little "barn" backdrop to film in front of. We borrowed a half dozen Christmas trees from friends and neighbors and hung lights all around to make it look nice. Then we just turned the cameras on and started filming.

The first half of the shoot was in the house, around the Christmas tree that Joey had set up (I was super excited because I love Christmas so much, and our tree went up in October that year) and also in the kitchen. We just let the cameras roll while we talked and set up each of the thirteen or fourteen songs that we had recorded and were about to film, performing them in the barn. It was kinda cheesy but mostly endearing.

We started getting ready at 6:00 a.m. and began filming at 9:00 a.m. Our hope was to be done filming everything by 4:00 p.m. We didn't even make it out to the barn to start filming the performances until 3:00 p.m. or so. So when Gabe finally yelled "Cut!" for the last time and "It's a wrap," we looked at our watches, and it was 5:00 a.m. We had been at it for almost twenty-four hours. We were beyond tired but also elated. When Joey and I climbed into the bed as the sun was coming up, we were both almost giddy. Partly because we were exhausted but also because we had done it. We'd really done it.

Bib & Buckle

Some signs are more than signs.

There is a sign painted on the exterior of our horse barn, just above the stalls, that reads "Bib & Buckle Fest." It's been there since late May 2013, and though it now seems random and doesn't make sense to keep it there, I can't seem to bring myself to paint over it.

Most people can't even see it. You'd have to be out in the cemetery or somewhere in our back field to know it's there. Ten feet high and probably thirty feet long, it stands out pretty good when I'm sitting on the bench beside my wife's cross. The horses chewing on hay just below it in a small, dry paddock.

The barn was originally a tobacco barn, or at least the posts that the horse barn was built on were. It sat down by the road, near where the entrance to the concert hall now is. But by the time I bought the farm, it was ancient, with roof tin missing and trees growing through the sides of it. Once filled floor to ceiling with tobacco grown here on the property, the barn kept the junk we had stored in there for the first five years or so of owning the place. My brother's old Impala, an engine puller, and a bunch of other things filled the dust-covered floor until we had Thomas disassemble the barn, piece by piece.

It probably took him two weeks or so to bring it down, keep what was salvageable and burn what wasn't. The dozen or so twenty-five-foot-tall cedar posts were hauled up the hill to a spot where we had chosen to build a horse barn. We had no real plans to get horses anytime soon, but we needed to use the cedar for something, and since I was always scheming to make my wife's dreams come true . . . a potential horse barn was what they became.

A lot has happened in that barn since then. Back when it was only posts and a roof with two large lean-tos on each side, it was where Heidi held her wedding reception. It has also stored mowers and tractors and hay and lumber and a thousand other things. Although one side would eventually become a tool barn and stay that way (it still is), the other side basically became the same thing it was before—a storage shed—only one hundred yards or so farther west and over the ridge, closer to the house.

But in the late spring of '13, it found its real purpose.

We had been having a hometown music festival here for years. Five years to be exact, I think. The next Bib & Buckle Festival was coming up, so we needed a place to hold it and a flat area to advertise it. Joey thought our new horse barn would do nicely, and it did.

We called it the Bib & Buckle Fest because of my bib overalls, of course, and the belt buckles Joey loved to wear with her jeans and western shirts. Looking back, I think it's kind of a silly name, but we liked it at the time, and, for the most part, it was easy for folks to remember. It was our way of giving back to the fans who were always so giving to us. After spending countless days each year traveling from state to state and town to town, playing for people in the places they lived, we wanted to invite them to spend a day with us. In the community and at the farm where we live.

People traveled from all over the country to come. Some from all over the world. Some were young families with lots of kids and babies still in diapers, and some were older folks and couples who'd been married longer than Joey and I'd been alive. People loved it, and so did we.

We held the first one about ten miles away at our friends Ben and

Debora Smith's farm. It was a year or so after our music career had taken off, and we probably had a couple hundred people show up. There was lots of music and another neighbor, Rex Wharton, cooked the brisket on his smoker, and Marcy Jo's provided the sides. We set up a volleyball net and horseshoe pits and lots of fun things for families to do, besides listening to us and some other musician friends that we'd invited to perform that day.

A year or two later we moved it to our farm, in our front yard, and had five hundred people there. Then the next year a thousand people showed up. When it finally got too big, we moved it into the back field; and the last year we held it, there were close to twenty-five hundred people in lawn chairs, with their feet tapping and their faces covered with sun-block. Being part of a day filled with music, food, and fun. Unfortunately, it rained cats and dogs that last year. Pretty much flooded us out about halfway through. But, in the end, it was our favorite festival of all. The one we remember most.

After hours of music through the late afternoon . . . around sunset, Joey and I would take the stage. When it was in the front of our farm-house, we performed on our front porch. The last year it was on a hay wagon parked beside the horse barn. Hay bales and string lights every-where, it was magical. A sea of people covered the back pasture from the barn to the cemetery. And hundreds of cars parked behind that.

The sign is beginning to show some signs of age now. But it's still beautiful. Each letter white with a black shadow, hand painted by Joey and her mama. I had created a festival logo in Photoshop on my computer and projected the image onto the barn in the dark, the night before, and traced the lines with a Sharpie. Joey and June had started in the early morning, the day before the festival, and finished the masterpiece by late evening.

That was the last festival we had here at the farm. For a few reasons. First off, the following year we took a break from music to have a baby, and the next summer we were fighting cancer and the year after that, fighting the deep heartbreak that comes with losing the one you love.

But through it all the sign has remained. A reminder of how beautiful life was. Of how beautiful life still is.

When Indy and I ride out into the back field on the Polaris Ranger, sometimes I let her climb into my lap and "drive" for a while. As she spins us in circles, giggling from ear to ear, I almost always find myself staring at the spot where Joey and her mama sat on the red tin with their cans and brushes in 2013, painting and talking. Wondering what it was they were saying to each other. An exciting weekend in front of them and not a care in the world . . . other than how to feed and handle having a couple thousand people that were about to converge on our little farm.

Our bus driver and good friend Russell Brisby would always say, "We Brisbys fear change," when Joey and I would ask him about making some improvement on the house or one of the barns. But, for some reason, Joey and I always seemed to welcome it. Knowing that from some change in our surroundings usually comes some kind of change within us.

There have been lots of changes since that day Joey and her mama climbed up onto the lean-to and painted those words. Some have been terribly hard to swallow or get used to, and some have been okay. And some changes don't seem like changes at all.

Joey's favorite belt buckle is still here. Laid out neatly on the nightstand beside our bed, it has a large "J + R" carved in silver with beautiful filigree and carvings around it. It was a gift from a cowboy we'd really only met once named Billy Hudson. I'd seen him wearing an unusually beautiful buckle at an event we were performing at in Alabama and mentioned how I'd like to get one like it for my wife . . . He showed up at our little family restaurant Marcy Jo's with Joey's buckle a couple months later.

I'm not sure if we ever even properly thanked him. But if he was paying attention to country music videos or award shows for the next seven or eight years afterward, I'm sure he's seen it. Joey loved that buckle and wore it to just about everything. It is one of the most prized possessions I have.

And I, of course, am still in my bib overalls. They grow a little tighter and looser, depending on whether I'm doing the cooking most of the time or my sisters are having us over for dinner a lot. I don't have as many of them as I used to own. Only a shelf with a half dozen pair in different colors now. I have a pair of jeans in my closet that I try on from time to time, but I've yet to wear them. I just keep rotating bibs and shirts. Always a little different but, somehow, still the same.

I think I'll just leave the sign there on the barn like it is. At least until the letters fade so much you can't read what it says anymore. Then maybe I'll get out the red paint and cover it up. But then again, maybe someday instead, I'll get the urge to put a fresh coat of white paint on those letters and park another hay wagon stage in front of the barn. Maybe even plug a guitar in and open the gate.

And see if anybody shows up.

Presidential Treatment

> "And I met the president of the
> United States . . . again."
>
> —Forrest Gump

We have some good friends who own the Texas Rangers, and from time to time Joey and I would go see a game with them. I have been to only a few major league baseball games in my life, so when I go see one with the owner of the team, it's kind of a different experience.

Joey had never been to a major league game before the first time we went to one at the Rangers' ballpark. We had been visiting our friends at their home in north Texas, and late in the afternoon when it was time to head to the game, we jumped in the car with them to go.

Soon we were sitting in a jet, and twenty minutes after that, we were getting back into an SUV headed the mile or so to the ballpark. Three motorcycle policemen were waiting for us when the plane touched down, and as we drove off the tarmac toward the stadium, they led the way. Sirens blaring and lights flashing. They stopped traffic in front of us, and we never even had to slow down. Driving through intersection after intersection, through what seemed like a sea of cars, all trying to get to the same place we were. It was clear that Texas is proud of their ball teams.

"This is just like the president," Joey whispered in my ear, as we crossed another intersection and people stopped and stared and waved. And it was. I had never seen anything like it.

A few minutes later our black SUV disappeared into the belly of the ballpark and up a ramp to the owner's parking spot. Some security men led us the few feet to a door that led to a hallway that led to the owner's box. We hadn't walked twenty steps when another door to the hallway opened up, and George W. Bush stepped in front us.

"Well, hello, Mr. President," our friend said.

"Hi, Ray," the president answered. "How're you doing?"

"I'd like to introduce you to some good friends of mine," our friend said, turning to Joey and me.

"This is Joey Feek." The president smiled at Joey and shook her hand.

"And this is her husband, Rory." The former president of the United States just sort of stared at me for a few seconds. I'd like to think that he recognized me from our TV shows or was a big fan of our music. But more realistically he was trying to figure out how I managed to marry such a beautiful woman. And also why a guy was in bib overalls at a Rangers game. And why was he friends with the owner?

He shook my hand and smiled. "Nice to meet you, Rory," he said. And he headed to his seat, and we headed to ours.

As we watched the game from high above the Rangers' dugout, drank, and ate the free food and ice cream to our heart's content, I turned to Joey, and she was smiling. "This is crazy, isn't it?" she said to me as she snuggled into my arm.

And it was. Just like our whole life and love story together was. And is. Filled with stories that are hard to believe but are true. Always pinching ourselves, saying, "Wow, isn't this something . . ." in the very hardest and the very best of times.

I Love You, I Love You, I Love You

. . . just say it.

My sister Marcy had never told me she loved me. She showed it to me and others in a thousand little ways, but she couldn't say it. Couldn't say the words. I'm not sure why. She just couldn't. For twenty years. Thirty years. She kept those words locked away inside.

I remember many times when something beautiful would take place and Marcy would so desperately want to say the words but couldn't get them to come out. Her face would turn red, and tears would fall, and she would open her mouth and try to speak them, but they wouldn't come. I would say, "It's okay . . . ," and her tears would fall harder but still nothing.

I guess something that happened in her life years and years ago . . . or many "somethings" . . . made her close that door and promise herself never to open it again. Hurt, I'm sure. Deep, deep pain that someone caused her. Everyone caused her.

And so the greatest three words in the English language stayed trapped inside of my sister for decades. Until the day finally came when the dam broke and the truth flooded out. I don't remember what happened. When that was exactly. What caused it. But I know it was about six or seven years ago. And Marcy's never been the same since.

Now, there isn't hardly a phone call we have or a text that she sends that doesn't end with "I love you." If Indiana and I walk over to visit in the afternoon so my baby can play with her grandbabies, it's almost guaranteed that she will tell Indy, "Aunt Marcy loves you," again and again while they're playing with dolls or puzzles. And before I get out the door to head home, she'll have hugged me and said the words to me too . . . *I love you.* It is so beautiful to see and hear. Especially knowing how long she had gone without being able to say those words.

We all have things that we long to say but don't. Powerful words and phrases that can change the world for someone, including ourselves.

I love you. I'm proud of you. I'm sorry. I forgive you.

Love that we want to show or share, but we keep it locked inside. Sometimes to protect ourselves for self-preservation or because we're damaged and we have desperately needed to hear someone say the words to us, but they never came . . . and so now we don't know how to say them to others.

And sometimes because we think there'll be lots of time to say the things we want to say to the people we care about. But the truth is, there isn't.

Losing my wife, Joey, made it painfully clear that none of us know what tomorrow holds or even if there's going to be a tomorrow for us. All there really is is today. Right now. And so I try my best to tell the people around me how much they mean to me, what a great job they are doing with their kids and with following their dreams, and that I love them. To swallow my own pride and build theirs a little bit with words today and not someday.

Almost every single Valentine's Day card, Father's Day card, or love letter or note that I ever received from my wife ended the same way.

I love you, I love you, I love you.

For Joey and me, it wasn't enough to say it once to each other, we always said it three times. It was originally a line in the chorus of a song called "Josephine" that I wrote before Joey and I got married. And, somehow, we adopted it, and it is how we said I love you to each other. Three times. Always.

And in my wife's final days, it was one of the last things she said to me. And in her final moments, kneeling beside her bed with her frail hand in mine . . . the last thing that I said to her . . .

I love you, I love you, I love you.

Modern Family

Like most families, ours is
functionally dysfunctional.

Joey and I saw only a couple episodes of the TV series *Modern Family*, and we thought it was super funny. Crazy but funny. I really enjoyed it because, like the family in the sitcom, my extended family is a bit of a mess. With dysfunction everywhere and a plethora of story lines and characters you would hardly believe are real. But they are.

And, at the same time, when the crazy meter seems pegged a little higher than it is with most families, like the one in the sitcom ours is a family with heart. A heart that is trying to be something better than it is. Something wonderful. And usually as a family unit, we fall somewhere between broken and beautiful.

Through the last fifty years, my brothers and sisters and I have loved each other. Hated each other. And spent a lot of years somewhere in between. We have been close. Far, far away. And mostly both at the same time. We have had moments when it feels like the same blood is running through our veins and other seasons when we're convinced that we must be adopted and from a family far different than our own.

I think my mother's way of dealing with the dysfunction in our family was to pretend. To imagine that we were an amazing, tight-knit group of siblings—always there for each other. It wasn't true most of the time, but for her, I think she needed it to be. Or maybe, just maybe, she wanted to believe it into existence. And you know what . . . over time, we are actually doing fairly well.

My two sisters live on each side of our property now. Marcy and her husband, Donny, on the south side and Candy and Keith on the north. Living this close to each other, we spend an unusual amount of time together, and, for the most part, it's incredible. I think we've learned to respect each other and to understand that we are all "doing the best we can with what we have," and that's made a big difference.

My brothers live together now, thirty or forty miles west of the farm, on a place where, like me, they are putting down roots. Trying to make a better life for themselves and their kids and grandkids. I don't see them that often, maybe every couple of months or so. But when I do, we give each other hugs and try to catch up on our lives. What's happening in their world and in mine. With their kids and mine.

We are all so alike. And yet completely different. Most of us have battled demons our whole lives. Some, like my youngest sister, Candy, have had a better grasp on it than the rest of us. She made good choices early in her life and has mostly seen the fruit of them. And others of us have meandering, broken paths that have led us from hardship to hardship to get to where we are today.

There have been countless glasses lifted up to cheer in the arrival of babies and countless trips to rehab centers. Lots of hopeful church altar weddings and almost as many frustrated courthouse divorces. Time spent in houses that felt like prisons and jail cells that provided the freedom to really think for the first time in a long time.

But through it all we have been a family. We are a family still. Modern and yet old-school. Trying to prepare for the future and keep grounded in the values of the past. We have come a long way, and we are clear that we still have a long way to go. But we're hopeful. Hopeful that we've learned from our mistakes and, even more so, that our children have learned from them. And that maybe, just maybe, they can enjoy a bit more of the good stuff of life together and have to endure less of the bad.

Our Very Own

My wife's dog, Rufus, was a star
long before Joey and I were.

When I married Joey, it was a two-for-one deal. She came with a dog. Not just a dog . . . a hound named Rufus.

Regal and handsome, Rufey was Joey's best friend and they went everywhere together. He was with her when we had our first "coffee date," and she was with him when the vet gave him a shot that relieved his arthritic pain once and for all.

He was a permanent fixture in the bed of her truck and by her side morning and night. And they had a bond like nothing I'd ever seen before. She only asked once, and he did everything she asked him to. He was obedient and sweet and a lot of fun too. Joey would tell him to start singing and he would start howling louder and louder for her and we would laugh and howl with him.

Somewhere around 2004, Joey was working at the horse vet clinic in Thompson Station and a producer for an upcoming movie came in looking for her. For Rufus, actually. He'd heard that Rufus would do just about anything Joey asked him to, and they needed a hound for a part in a movie they were about to start shooting.

"Will he ride on a car?" he asked Joey.

"He rides in the back of my truck all the time," Joey said.

"But will he ride on top of a car . . . on the roof of one . . . while it's going down the road?" he asked again.

"He can do it," Joey answered.

And just like that, Rufus was cast in a movie. It was called *Our Very Own*. You can see it on Netflix or buy the DVD on Amazon. Rufus is on the movie poster.

That evening, Joey told me about the movie producer, and within a few minutes I had my old '56 Buick in the yard, with a rug on the top. Joey said, "Up, Roo . . ." and Rufus climbed up the trunk and stood on top of the roof.

"Stay," was all she said. And he did.

I drove in circles around our farmhouse, with Joey's hound on the roof of my car, and he just kept his eyes on his "mama" and never moved a muscle.

"Let's see how he does on the road," Joey said. And a few minutes later I was sitting in the Buick on the lane that goes behind our house, and Rufus was on the car again.

"Stay, Rufey." She looked at me and said, "Take it slow, honey." And I headed down the lane away from her with a dog on the top of my car. I'm sure the neighbors thought we'd lost our minds.

He was still on the car, staring at Joey as we went over the rise and out of sight. I turned around and drove back with him still there. When I pulled up next to my wife, she was grinning ear to ear.

"Isn't that something . . . ," she said with a big smile. "Good boy, Roo." She motioned for him to come, and he ran down the hood and went straight to her side.

The following weekend we were all at the movie set in Shelbyville, a small town an hour or so away from where we lived. It was the first time we'd ever been on a movie set, and it was all pretty neat to take in. Camera crews and gear everywhere. Catering trucks and tents and people gathered around, watching. Hoping to get a glimpse of a couple of the well-known actors who had flown in from Hollywood to play key roles in the film.

They were going to be filming a few of Rufus's scenes that day, and the director and producers of the movie greeted us when we arrived and treated Rufus like a star. One of them had grown up in the town and had been dreaming of making this movie for years, and he said that Rufus's role was an important one. The story was loosely based on his teenage years and an event that happened in their small town. He said that an old man who lived in the town back then had a dog that rode in the back of his truck everywhere he went, but when his truck broke down and he had to drive his wife's car, he had a dilemma. She wouldn't let his beloved dog ride inside, so the man taught him to climb on top of the car, and that's how they traveled. And if you were living and walking around the town back in the '70s, the filmmakers said, you would see the car come by almost daily with this dog riding on the roof.

And so Rufus was cast to play the old man's dog, and that afternoon and evening was when the cameras were going to start rolling to capture the scenes that Rufey would be in.

By late afternoon a large crowd had gathered in the town square to watch the filming. The director told Joey to see if her dog would stand on the little blue car as it drove down the street and past a movie theater. Joey smiled and said, "No problem."

I think they did it in one take.

The cameras were rolling when the car drove past the actors who were standing on the sidewalk talking and turned to go down the street and out of sight. The director yelled, "Cut!" and the whole crew started applauding and high-fiving. It was so fun to see and be a part of. As the car came to a stop, Rufey just stayed where he was, taking in all the sights and sounds and not moving an inch till Joey rubbed his ears and said, "Down, boy."

They filmed a couple more scenes where the car came driving by with the dog on it, and then our big day was over.

A year or so later we came to the premiere, and they gave us all hats that they'd made up with the production company logo on it. Their logo was a dog on a car. It was pretty special. Rufus took pictures with the stars and even walked the red carpet with my bride. It was a day we would never forget.

I'd never seen a dog who loved someone as much as Rufus loved Joey. Or an owner who loved a dog as much as she did him. A number of years later, after Rufus passed away, Joey got another puppy that we named Ranger, who grew up to be just like Rufey. Though he was a completely different breed—smaller, with much more fur—he was almost like the exact same dog. He loved Joey with all his heart and would do just about anything she asked him to do.

Ranger's seven years old now. Still just as smart and obedient for me as he was for my bride. Maybe I need to pull my '54 Oldsmobile into the yard and put a rug on top of her, and see if Ranger wants to take a ride.

Heartlight

We auctioned ourselves off . . .
and it changed our lives.

It was a sold-out event. A fund-raiser for Heartlight, a teens-at-risk ministry in Texas that was started and is run by a friend of ours named Mark Gregston. Joey and I were the special entertainment for the evening, and we performed after the dinner while the silent auction was going on.

The show had gone well, and we were done. Sitting at our table about to pick up a glass of wine and enjoy ourselves for a little while. But something told me we should do more. Give more. Joey thought so too. So I called the auctioneer over.

Within a few minutes we were back up on the stage but this time with the auctioneer, and he was taking bids on us. We had decided to auction ourselves off. We would come anywhere and play a show for the highest bidder. It wasn't like us to do something like that because we had been on the road traveling so much and were tired and just wanted to be home. Besides, you never know where you might end up, and once you commit, there's no going back.

The next few minutes were a blur. Folks bidding and the number rising. I think someone paid fifteen thousand dollars for us that evening, and when it was over, Joey was looking at me like, "What have we done?" But we loved our friend Mark and knew that he was doing amazing work there for struggling teenagers, and the money they raised would be helpful.

"Rory and Joey . . . I'd like you to meet the woman who purchased you," Mark said. And a tall, pretty lady with a newborn in her arms said, "Hello, I'm Kris." Both my wife and I immediately liked her and knew all would be fine.

"My parents have a wedding anniversary, and my mom loves you guys . . . and I thought I'd surprise them and have you come sing for their party."

Joey and I had no idea who this lady was or who her parents were.

We found ourselves on an airplane a few weeks later, headed back to Texas to sing at a party. When we got to the place where we were singing, it was at a very beautiful home north of Dallas. And the party was downstairs, in a basement area in one of their guest quarters. But there were only about a dozen people there. Maybe less. It was just the couple and a few other couples from their church that they were close friends with. We ate barbecue and visited and loved every one of them immediately. Then we sang a few songs. We didn't need a microphone or PA system, we just gathered our chairs in a circle and sang for them.

A few songs later they started singing for us. Old hymns. Joey loved it so much. And she loved them, especially the couple we were there to sing for. We both did.

In the coming months and years, we became close friends and made many trips back to see them, or they would make trips to come see us play. Me becoming closer to the man, who would become more of a father figure to me than anyone in the last twenty years, and Joey growing closer to his wife.

We are still friends. They mean the world to us. Because they have changed our lives.

They are the ones who stepped in and funded the crazy idea I had of making a weekly television show at home and saw to it that our dream of turning the story of Josephine into a movie became a reality.

It is amazing to think that when we raised our hand that evening and gave ourselves away, we had no idea God would use that moment to bring some very special people into our lives who would change everything for us. For our careers.

And not just our careers. Our hearts and our lives.

When Joey was recovering from her cancer surgery, they brought their plane to the hospital to pick us up and bring us home, so Joey didn't have to make the long drive home from Chicago. And they have continued to care and love on us and be here for us through it all. Like ours, their tears have never stopped falling for the loss of Joey.

A few weeks before we found out that the chemo and radiation weren't working and decided to stop treatments, we were in Texas performing at another fund-raiser. Joey was very weak but loved her time on stage and was thankful for the chance, for thirty minutes or so, to take her mind off all she'd been through and just sing and tell our story.

The same lady who bought us, Kris, was in the audience. As were her parents and a number of the folks who'd been at the original fund-raiser and anniversary dinner where we sang. In tears, Joey and I told the story about how we had nervously given ourselves away years before and had received so much more in return than we ever dreamed. And when the show was over, dozens—maybe hundreds—of men in the audience gathered around us and laid their hands on my sweet bride and prayed for a miraculous healing of her body. We held each other and cried and cried.

I think our friends are crying still. Missing Joey. Wishing that miracle had come true. But both she and I knew that another miracle had already happened. That they were our miracle.

Thank you, Ray and Linda, we love you.

Bare-Metal Truth

The truth hurts . . . but it mostly makes me smile.

Russdriver, as we affectionately call him, has got a gift and it's not just driving and fixing buses, although he's pretty darn good at those things too.

The first old car I tinkered with in the new barn was a 1956 Buick I had bought from a parking lot for three hundred dollars. It was white and orange . . . the orange was actually spots where the years of sitting out in the rain had turned the metal to rust or, in a lot of places, had eaten right through the metal, and there were gaping holes in the car. The interior was in even worse shape than the body, and that's saying a lot. But I had big dreams of fixing her up and taking my bride to the drive-in and having people knock on the window and point and say, "Man, what a beautiful ride."

Unfortunately, what I didn't have much of was experience and skills when it came to fixing and restoring old cars. I had none, actually. But now I had a shop and a bunch of new tools and some time on my hands. So I rolled up my sleeves and started in. Mostly sanding. The first thing I did was strip everything off the car and start trying to sand her down to bare metal. My hope was to have her ready to paint in a couple weeks.

But days of sanding turned into weeks, and still there was a ton left to do. I had a couple of the fenders done, and that's about it when the time came for Joey and me to go back out on the road. When Russell pulled up in the big tour bus, I showed him the progress I'd made on the car and told him about my big dreams. We loaded up, and as we were about to head out, I saw Thomas, our farmhand and handyman at the farm, feeding our cow. The weather was beginning to drop below freezing, and there wasn't much for him to do on the farm for the next week or two, so I mentioned to him, if he found himself with some spare time, not to be afraid to pick up a sander and see if he could make any headway.

Ten days later the tour bus pulled back into the farm with Joey and I thankful to have a series of shows out in the Midwest completed and ready to be back home for a while. As we unloaded our clothes and guitars from the bus, I walked into the shop area of the big barn and saw my Buick sitting there. The whole thing had been sanded down to shiny metal. Every inch of it. I called out to Russ and Joey to come look.

"Wow!!!" Russell said, as he walked around looking at the bumper-to-bumper bare metal, and Joey stood by my side smiling. "You know you've made it when you can hire someone to do your hobbies for you!!"

Joey started laughing, and so did I. I didn't want to, but I couldn't help it. Russ always has a way of boiling a situation down to the bare-metal truth. He always has.

One time, a couple years later, when I was trying to figure out if I should join a gym to start working out or not, I asked Russell what he thought I should do. I felt like I needed to do something since I was getting older and needed to take better care of myself. But the closest gym was a pretty good drive away, and I'd have to pay a monthly fee to work out there, and usually you don't follow through on it . . . and on and on my concerns went.

"You're brilliant," he said. "While other people are paying money each month to pick up some heavy things from one spot and move them to another . . . you have all these rocks and firewood here at your farm. You are able to pick them up and move them around for free!"

I didn't much like his answer at the time, but it was true. I did have lots of ten- and twenty- and fifty-pound rocks and logs and bags of feed that I could just pick up and work out with here at the farm. And it wasn't really even working out, it was just called working. The way that people have kept themselves in good shape for the history of time, before the gym and fitness industry came in and changed how we look at things.

I love our bus driver Russell so much. But he is wrong about one thing . . . I'm not the brilliant one. Russ is. He knows just what to say and when to say it, to make you see things in a new and better light.

Brand - New Bus

We've never had a brand-new bus. But
then again, we have. Many, many times.

Joey and I only owned two tour buses in our lives and music career together, and they both were old. One was ancient, built in 1955, and the other was more of a middle-aged coach that we named Coach, and it came rolling off the assembly line in 1990. They'd each had a million or more miles of hauling hard-living dreamers and band members up and down the highways of America, long before they hauled us and our dogs, Rufus and then Ranger, and, in time, our baby girl, Indiana.

Joey and I loved those buses and the history that came with them. The '55 had been a passenger bus back in the day. I got it from a man in Canada who'd got it from God knows how many other men who got it from other men. Somewhere along the line someone turned it into a tour bus with bunks and a small kitchen and living area. The fella I got it from, John Foot, had recently given her a new paint job. And though I didn't have as much money as he was asking for her in my pocket when we arrived at his house after an eight-hour drive north from Indiana, he took what I had and decided my handshake was good for the rest, and it was.

My father-in-law and brother-in-law went with me to look at it that day in '05. Not just to look at it but to pick it up. You can't make a drive that far and say, "I'll go home and think about it." You've got to think fast and make a decision. My thinking ended with Joey's daddy and me driving across the Canadian border at about two in the morning with no title or papers saying we owned it and my brother-in-law behind us in his SUV. The authorities just looked at us in the office that night, then out the border office window at the bus, then back at us and the bus again. Then, for some reason, said, "Okay, you're good to go," and let us cross the bridge and try to make it back to Tennessee or however far we were gonna get before it broke down. I figure they must've just felt sorry for us. For the drive and the future in front of us with the old girl.

I dropped off Joey's daddy, Jack, at his house in Indiana in the early morning and pulled into our driveway late that afternoon. My eyes about as bloodshot as my nerves. Joey met me in the driveway. Skeptical but with a big smile and a cup of coffee. "She's beautiful," Joey said as she hugged me, like I'd just bought something wonderful instead of the death trap that it was.

Like I had with the other old cars in the barn, I had visions of fixing her up and driving my wife around the country, going from radio station to radio station, trying to get the DJs to play Joey's beautiful songs so people could hear them. I sorta saw myself like Loretta Lynn's husband, Doolittle, in the movie *Coal Miner's Daughter*. But before we ever got to a radio station, the bus broke down and left us stranded on the side of the interstate. We called for help, and my sister picked up Joey and took her home. I stayed with the bus till a wrecker came . . . about four hours later. Freezing to death, with no heat and no way to start the bus to stay warm, as car after car stopped, I waved them on, saying, "No, I'm okay; there'll be a wrecker along soon."

It was the middle of the night when we finally pulled into the driveway with me riding shotgun in the wrecker and the bus being drug, literally, behind. She was in bad shape, and my spirits were at rock bottom. The bus stayed parked for months and months. Till another wrecker came and took it to a shop that said, "We can fix it, but it'll cost ya." By then Joey wasn't so gracious. The beautiful old girl was becoming a bit of a nightmare and a money pit. So there she sat. Until Russ came along, that is.

Russdriver owned a couple of other buses, and by this time, Joey's and my music career had taken off with a bang. We were traveling all across the country, going from radio station to station, and show to show. All pretty much on airplanes. My wife wanted off the planes and onto a bus. A real bus. And so Russ leased one to us one weekend, then he drove us to some shows in another bus he had a few weeks later. Not long after, he was sitting at our kitchen table and going through the numbers with me, trying to see if we could afford to lease a bus for a few months and not have to fly anymore. It's what Joey desperately wanted and what I wanted to make happen for her.

After some quick figuring, his smile turned to a frown, and he showed me how the numbers were never gonna work. He stood up to shake my hand and leave, but, for some reason, I got a crazy idea in my head.

"We got an old bus," I said. "Since we can't afford you or a nice bus . . . is there any chance you might help us fix up the one we have and travel with us . . . as part of our family?"

Now, Russ has a million-dollar smile, and, all of a sudden, his face was filled with it.

"I'm in," he said, as he shook my hand. And that was that. Russdriver was part of the family. And the family had commitments to make, and Mama wanted to drive to them.

And so we and Russ and our handyman, Thomas, got the bus back to the farmhouse and started fixing it up. We got her running and then gutted it and put in a couch and a glider and a coffee maker so it would feel like home. Joey made curtains, and we even put in a desk so I could work as we drove down the road. Home but not at home. That was the goal. And we hit it.

That doesn't mean it didn't break down now and then or that we didn't have to run alongside of it with a stick pointed at the gearbox and Russell yelling, "Now!" as loud he could so we could get it into second gear and I could jump in and we could head to a festival in Sheboygan, Wisconsin, or a show at a military base in Aberdeen, Maryland, or some place in between.

We spent some time on the side of highways and backed into garages in places like Beulah, Wyoming, and Hiawatha, Kansas. But, for some reason, those things were fun to Russell. He lived for problems that would come our way in the old bus. If the lights started to dim as we headed down Monteagle Mountain in the middle of the night, he'd say, "Generator's failing . . . next exit's eighteen miles . . . this is gonna get exciting!" And we'd go flying down the mountainside with no lights on and him *so* excited to get to an exit and pull out his toolbox and try to troubleshoot the problem. And he always did. I don't know how, but he did. We never missed a show or a station visit. Never even late for one.

But that wasn't the amazing part. It was when we got back in the bus that the magic happened. He would fire it up and yell, "Wahoo!! It's a brand-new bus." And he meant it. That's how he saw it. It was different now. What we were driving down the road from that moment on wasn't what he had before. It was better. Way better. Perfect, actually.

And he wasn't just that way with our old tour buses, he was that way with everything. Anything. One little improvement, and it was a whole new thing. Or a whole new person. Yesterday melted away, and all there was was right now, and right now is amazing! What a gift Russ has.

But the best part of all is that it's contagious. Soon Joey and I felt the same way about the bus and about every other bump in the road that we faced. Just a little improvement, and it was a brand-new situation.

I believe that Russell, and how he sees life, had an influence on Joey and is part of why she looked at things with so much positivity when she was going through her battle with cancer. And why I see the good in life now after so many tough things have happened.

We sold our 1990 tour bus, Coach, in 2015, when Joey's cancer came back. Actually, Russ sold it for us.

We didn't have any need for it anymore, and, besides, with all the medical expenses that were being racked up, we could use the money.

And though Russ was now technically out of a job with us . . . he never stopped working for us. I would suspect it's because if you asked him, his job wasn't driving a tour bus . . . it was loving us and taking care of us. Bus or no bus. And he was, and is, brilliant at his job.

He helped us fix up our old 1955 bus and hauled us all across the country with no power steering and no A/C when our career was just getting started. And when we moved up to a 1990 Silver Eagle a few years later, he was still behind the wheel. Still driving all night, getting to gigs and setting up merchandise for us, sound-checking our guitars and taking pictures for fans at meet and greets. He was also making sure that Joey had something healthy to eat in a hundred green rooms all across the country. All he was being paid to do was drive; the rest of it was because he loved us. And because he was part of our family. He still is.

Now, here it is a couple years later, and I see Russdriver almost every day next door at my brother-in-law Keith's house . . . he's been in the big barn working on a bus. A new old bus. And not just any bus.

Our bus.

He found one for us that he's been fixing up. Like me, it's got a bit of history (to put it mildly) and could use a new story to tell. It was rusting out and deserted in a parking lot when Russ found it—nothing much to look at—but it was actually quite famous at one time.

She was the old *Girls Gone Wild* bus that you may have seen on TV twenty years ago, going from town to town, picking up pretty girls that, well . . . went wild.

But by the time Russell found her, she was broken down and abandoned and not worth much of anything. Russ being who Russ is . . . bought her and is fixing her up. Actually, a couple weeks ago he moved her out into the bus barn here at the farm. He and his buddy Ray spend the days sanding down the rust and peeling paint, getting it ready not just for new paint but for a new story.

A couple months ago, when Russ first told me about this bus, I thought it was crazy that he bought one with a sordid history as this one had. But not long after that, Aaron and I spent an afternoon with Russell ripping out the old carpet and listening to him dream about what the bus could be, and his excitement about it moved me, and I sat down that evening and wrote this:

I was young, what can I say? I didn't know any better. My family wanted me to do something respectful for a living . . . maybe drive around from college to college filled with important medical equipment, like my ol' man did. Or drive a nice couple and their dog around, like my grandfather, the Coach, did. But I was rebellious, like all youngsters are. I wanted to take my own road.

His name was Joe, and he was a smooth talker. Said he'd show me the world and make me famous. Even put me on TV. How could I refuse? So I went with him, and for a while I felt pretty. People saw me coming and pointed and stared. Man, I was something. But life in the fast lane started to catch up with me. And some bad things happened. Things I'm not proud of. I didn't mean for it to. I just got caught up in the money and the drugs and the sex. Pretty soon I was old before my time. Used up and tossed to the side of the road. I felt so ashamed.

Joe moved on to someone else. First, a fancier Prevost, then a Leerjet, and then God-knows-what after that. Last I heard, he lost it all and was in hiding somewhere. In the meantime I was abandoned and forgotten. I ended up in an empty parking lot in Tennessee. For years nobody even looked at me. And if they did, they just made fun or threw rocks at me. I wanted to die. I almost did too.

But then, a few months ago . . . this nice man Russell came to look at me. And he saw something that no one else did. Through the rust and filth, he said, he saw something beautiful. And so he picked me. Out of every other one in the world, he picked me. Can you believe that? Not just that . . . he fought for me. He had to get a lawyer and fight to get custody of me.

And now . . . now he's fixing me up. He's making me feel brand-new again. I thought I was done . . . one step away from being scrapped and never heard from again. But, instead, he's making me a whole new bus. Or at least he's making me feel like I am. I'm still pretty rough if you look at me, but I'm getting there. I've got some new carpet and some blinds, and I'm even gonna get a fresh paint job soon. Who would do that for somebody like me? I know, it's crazy, right?

I'm so lucky. And the other day . . . I heard him say that I'm gonna get to drive around a man and his little baby and some other friends of Russell's. Wouldn't my mom and dad be so proud if they could see me now?

Who would've thought . . . just when all hope was lost. I get to start all over. We all need a fresh start. I can't wait to see what happens next.

It's silly, but that story made me cry when I wrote it. Just imagining what the bus might say if she could talk. But as much as it moved me, what moved me even more is Russ's plan for her. He wants her to be an angel bus.

Yes, we're gonna spend some time taking her out as a family. Maybe we'll even take her on a book tour next spring when this book comes out. Russ and the baby and me, going from town to town, like we used to do with Indy's mama. And we'll probably play some music and some shows at some point, but Russell's real hope, and mine too, is for it to help people who need it. To be a blessing to some kids and some adults who could use a blessing in their lives.

You see, when Joey got sick—really sick—since we had sold ours, Russell would borrow buses from other entertainers who owned them to pick up my wife and take her where she needed to go. Whether that was to the Cancer Treatment Center or home to Indiana to stay. And when Joey could no longer travel and hospice was brought in, Russell brought up a busload of Joey's friends from Tennessee to say goodbye to her. And after Joey passed and we had the funeral here at the farm, Russ took Indy and me and some of our family back up to Indiana in one of those buses to speak at a memorial service where a thousand people had gathered in her high school gymnasium to honor her and her life.

Russ blessed us greatly. And his hope is to keep that up and bless others in the same way.

That, in time, the new old bus could be used to take sick children and their families to and from the hospital. Maybe take someone home when they can't travel by car anymore and a million other needs that could be met. And, who knows, maybe that one bus could start a movement and turn into a dozen others doing the same thing all across the country.

You never know what might happen. Right now, I just know it's a beautiful thing that Russ is doing. Giving that old girl a chance to be part of a better story. And by doing that, it's giving us a chance to be part of a better story too.

Speak Love

Tell people you love them . . .
use words if you have to.

They say there are five love languages, and we all don't speak the same one. I believe that's true. At least it always has been in our house.

My wife's love language was "acts of service." It was how she said "I love you" and how she heard it also. Mine, on the other hand, is probably "physical touch." Maybe because I'm a boy, and boys are just wired to put a little extra emphasis on the language you speak when the lights are off. But it's more than that. I'm a hugger, and you'd be hard-pressed to find any moment of any day that you were around us when I didn't have my wife's hand in mine.

Joey's hand, on the other hand, was fine all by itself. But she loved me, and so hers reached for mine all the time too. I also said "I love you" to her a dozen times a day. She probably didn't need to hear it, but she knew I did, so she would say it back to me. Say it before I said it to her. She was telling me that she loved me in the languages that I understood.

She, on the other hand, needed to see the trash taken out and my dirty socks put in the clothes hamper. They weren't things that meant much of anything to me, but to her, when I did them, I wasn't just marking them off a to-do list that she had for me, I was saying "I love Joey." And so I became pretty good at saying "I love you," without saying "I love you." I tried to figure out what she wanted done that day, and I would get to it before she asked me. Before she even thought of it sometimes. And her smile made the work so, so worth it.

Our children spoke other love languages. And when you're a teenager, it's hard to see outside the little bubble that you're in . . . and early on in our marriage, Heidi wasn't feeling loved by Joey, and Joey wasn't feeling loved or respected by Heidi. I remember a time when Heidi was about sixteen, it all came to a head.

They were struggling to build a relationship. Joey and I had been married a year or two, but time hadn't made it better, only worse. Heidi needed Joey to be a friend more than a mother. Someone who would listen to her talk about her day at school and the girls who had said this and boys who had done that. But those were all trivial things that didn't appeal to Joey. There was so much to do around the house and in life, she thought that they were a waste of precious time. It's funny. To one person that is precious time, and to the other it's a waste of it.

We were all sitting in the living room—not talking—with a heaviness hanging over the room and the whole house. I had recently read the book *The Five Love Languages* by Gary Chapman, and, for some reason, it clicked inside of me—what was going on, what was really happening. Joey and Heidi were both screaming, "I love you!" to each other, but neither could hear it. Because they spoke completely different love languages.

Joey was cooking amazing dinners for us and keeping the house beautiful and doing laundry and a million other things . . . that to her said "I love you" to Heidi and Hopie and me. All she needed in return from the girls was for them to make their beds. To keep up their rooms and to pick up after themselves around the house. Heidi's room was a mess, which translated to "I don't love you" to Joey.

But Heidi couldn't hear the words that Joey's actions were saying because she didn't speak that language. And when she would try to pour her thoughts and feelings out to Joey, and Joey didn't respond by sitting down and saying, "Tell me all about it" . . . what she heard was Joey saying "I don't love you."

I told them about the book I read and how it seemed like there was a serious language barrier. Though they both listened, neither responded or changed anything right away. But in time they did come to realize what the other person wanted and needed, and they started talking the same language.

From then on, I don't remember Joey and Heidi having any real relationship issues that were insurmountable. They still had their moments, but, for the most part . . . they were both on the same page . . . still speaking other languages . . . but at least being aware of it and trying to bridge the gap between them.

With Hopie it was much the same. Though she's never told me, I feel certain that her love language is "words of affirmation." She longs to hear that she is doing a good job, words of encouragement, and that we approve of her. Unfortunately, again, at times that was very difficult for Joey and me to give Hopie. She always struggled with her organizational skills. And it is easy to withhold your approval if someone can't or doesn't do things the way that you think they should do them. I wish we had been more encouraging to Hopie through those teen years and into her early adulthood. It is something that I am working hard on today. Letting her know that I love her and support her, no matter what choices she makes or down what path she decides to go. And it's been so good for me to learn to speak her language. Giving love unconditionally creates the best condition for love to grow. It's just the way it works.

An outtake from the photo shoot for this book

The farmhouse when we bought it in 1999

The farmhouse today

Little Joey in overalls

Christmas morning with my first guitar

Photo by Aloosina Toomalatai

Wendy, Hopie, Heidi, and Dillon
playing cards at Heidi's house in Alabama

Joey at her high school graduation

Hopie and Heidi with me at the farm just before Joey came into our lives

Heidi singing "Daddy What If" with her dad on stage in Texas, 1990s

Hopie and Heidi next to the 1956 Chevy Bel Air we drove to Nashville when we moved in 1995

The girls by the restored Bel Air the day I gave it to them in May 2017

Our wedding day, June 15, 2002

Walking Joey down the
aisle . . . Joey was so beautiful

Putting on our work boots right after the wedding

With fifteen Dr. Pepper cans tied to the back of my '56 Chevy

With Blake Shelton at the #1 party
for "Some Beach," 2004

The Grammy Award we won
for the *Hymns* album

Joey and me singing for the first time
on stage at the Grand Ole Opry

Joey and me on CMT's *Can You Duet*, March 2008

Joey with baby ducklings at springtime

Joey loved being in her garden

Joey was so excited about the potting
house I gave her on her thirtieth birthday

One of our first Christmas
pictures together as a family

At the family cemetery on the farm, April 2010

Joey's greatest joy was the day Indiana was born

On the beach in Hawaii, January 2015

Our little ray of sunshine

Saying goodbye to the girls was one of the hardest things Joey had to do

Indiana and me outside the farmhouse, fall 2017

Potty "choo-choo" training Indiana

The one-room schoolhouse we're building at the farm

Hopie, Indy, Heidi, and me, fall 2017

Missing Joey—this is the same spot in the cemetery behind our farmhouse where we filmed our *When I'm Gone* video a few years earlier

Miss Congeniality

She lost, and she won.

When Heidi was in the ninth grade, she entered a local beauty contest. It was held on the theater stage at the middle school and Joey and I showed up to support her. We had no idea what we were in for.

A few minutes into it, Joey and I realized that the pageant was rigged. Not by the parents or the judges. But rigged in the way that life is rigged.

What suddenly became clear to us was that everyone isn't created equal. At least when it comes to beauty. I'm not sure what I thought or even if it had occurred to me until then, but it turns out that beauty isn't in the eye of the beholder. It is in the genes. It became clear that if your parents had high cheekbones and olive skin and a bunch of other characteristics that the world says are beautiful, then you just won the beauty contest lottery. Everybody else is screwed.

Strangely, there in that auditorium full of parents and kids, I became highly aware of myself. My freckles and fair skin and my difficult childhood . . . and as beautiful as Heidi and Hopie were, I didn't want them to be judged by something that I wasn't able to give them. Something inside of me wished that we weren't there. That Heidi wasn't there.

But my worries were for nothing. It turned out that Heidi didn't care at all about the beauty contest. The contest had a talent portion of the show, and she said she was there only to sing. For her, it was as simple as that. She wanted the chance to get on a stage and perform the song "What If God Was One of Us?" Which, it turns out, was the perfect song for that situation. What if God was one of us? . . . was a good question in the midst of a bunch of parents and kids worried about who is the most beautiful and who isn't. A great one, actually.

As Heidi stood on stage singing, Joey and I couldn't have been prouder.

In the end, our daughter walked away with the title of Miss Congeniality, which is funny because if you look *congeniality* up in the dictionary, it says, "the quality of being pleasant and friendly." Which was easy for Heidi to do since she was there only to sing.

So even though she didn't win, in her mind and ours, she won the whole thing.

Hymn and Her

She and hymn were a powerful combination.

There's a Grammy Award sitting on our mantel downstairs. It has both of our names on it, but it's there because of Joey.

My wife had dreamed of recording an album full of the hymns she grew up singing in church as a little girl. The songs her mama sang to her. That her grandmama sang to her mama.

And in the summer of 2015, we went in the studio and recorded that album. It was called *Hymns That Are Important to Us*, and we recorded the whole thing in one day. Every track and every overdub of the instruments happened that day at Larry Beaird's studio in Berryhill, a small enclave of houses and studios on the south side of Nashville.

It wasn't one of our best albums. Not by a long way. The arrangements were simple and the tracks weren't that unique. If you compare it to our album *Life of a Song* that Carl Jackson produced or *His & Hers* that Gary Paczosa produced, this one lacks something . . . well, pretty much everything. Those records are masterful. The production, the playing, the arrangements, the mixing . . . all of it. I can listen to them for days and days and never hear a flaw, not one.

The *Hymns* record, on the other hand, was about as flawed as they come. But in another way, it was filled with a magic the other albums didn't have.

Some of it is luck. Bad luck, to be exact. Though we had gone out on endless radio and marketing tours for the other albums we made, hoping that they would get traction and the songs would get some airplay and the stores would carry them and people would buy them, this one had none of that. We just made it and shared it. That's pretty much it.

Instead of trying to sell a record, we were busy trying to save a life. And sharing the whole thing with the world as we went through it. In the end, we sold a gazillion of the *Hymns* record. A half million of them, actually, and it has been a tremendous blessing for our family. For our family's family. And in February 2017, I found myself, along with my father-in-law and our coproducer, Joe West, standing on a stage at the Grammy Awards being handed *the* greatest honor a musician can receive. It was surreal, to say the least.

And now that award is on the mantel, and my wife's photos line the walls of our home. Only the hymns remain. Just as most of them have done for the past hundred and some years. They are timeless. Each one of them. "I Surrender All," "It Is Well with My Soul," "The Old Rugged Cross," and almost a dozen others that are listed on the back of the CD jacket.

Those songs have moved mountains for us. And God knows how many other mountains for others. They comforted my bride as her precious life slipped away and they comfort the baby and me as we drive down the road to school each morning, wondering what lies in store. The CD has basically been in our truck for eighteen months nonstop. I listen and think. And the baby sings along. At first only a word or two . . . that's all she knew. Not of the songs, but in general. But here lately, she's singing a lot of the words. She knows them, like her mama knew them. They are getting inside her, just like they were inside her mama.

Like they're inside me now.

Most of the songs I was only vaguely familiar with, if at all, before Joey came into my life. I wasn't raised around hymns, being a child of a

Catholic mother who only really went to church on Easter when it fell on a leap year. Not really, but that's about how often we went. At first glance the songs are simple. Not much to them. Boring, actually, or so I thought. But being a songwriter, the more I heard them, the more I read along in the pew as my wife sang them, the more I started to realize that they aren't simple at all. They are profound. Profoundly profound, actually.

I am a word guy. Mostly a lyric man when it comes to songwriting. And the words in most of the hymns that have stood the test of time have stood that test for darn good reason. Because they're amazing. They say so, so much, with so few words.

For years my wife would sit in the pew at church and cry along. She'd be singing, but tears would fill her eyes as she did. I understand why now. That's how I sing them. I cry along just as she did. And they wash the pain away. And the hurt and the worry, and they leave something else. Hope. Hope that there's more than what we see. Than what we can understand down here on earth.

And hope that I will see my beautiful bride again someday. Some heavenly day. And the angels will be singing her hymns. And together, we will cry along and keep an eye on our sweet girls below.

Uncle Dale

My three-thousand-dollar free guitar.

We call it Uncle Dale.

It's a 1963 Gibson Southern Jumbo guitar, and it came to me just as dramatically as it left me.

We named it after my father's younger brother Dale. He, like my dad, played guitar and sang—mostly songs by Merle Haggard, his hero. I didn't know Uncle Dale well, and I only remember being around him once, when I was young. Dad and I made a trip to Colorado to visit him and some other family that my father had there. I'm not exactly sure what year that would have been . . . the early 1970s, I think. I must've been around eight years old, and I don't know why it was just us on that trip, but it was.

We spent a day or two visiting Uncle Dale and his family, and then Dad took me to Estes Park, and I got to ride my first go-kart, which ended with me crashing into some tires and crying and him picking me up and us going out for ice cream.

In late 2008, not long after Joey's and my music career took off, I got an e-mail from Uncle Dale's wife, Linda. She said that he was really sick and that he'd been watching us and was so proud of me. And she sent me some wonderful pictures they had of Uncle Dale and my father when they were both young.

We kept in touch through the years, and sometime after he passed away, I got a call from his wife who said that she had Uncle Dale's guitar and wanted to know if I'd like to have it. I told her that I'd be honored, and so she sent it to me.

I had never owned an old guitar before, especially one that had any family history, so it was especially special for me. And it was also beautiful. I told Joey all about it and started playing it in the shows we played.

A few weeks later I got a call from my aunt, who said, "Did you ever research to see how much the guitar is worth?" . . . and then said something about how the roof on the trailer she's living in was leaking and the money would sure help her.

Well, I felt terrible. For two reasons. First off, that she had probably said something to me about finding out the value, and in my excitement I completely missed it. And secondly, I realized that I was going to have to pay her for it . . . and when I looked up the value of that model on the Internet, it said it was worth about three thousand dollars. Now, this didn't come in a time when we had the money to spare, so asking my wife if I could send a check for three thousand dollars for a guitar that I told her was free wasn't something that I was looking forward to.

But Joey was gracious and understood that we needed to help my aunt, and so we sent the check out, and I have played the guitar in most of our shows since then.

I played that guitar in the last show we performed, as a matter of fact. It was in Heber City, Utah, at the Cowboy Poetry Gathering in October 2016. We were all in Indiana with Joey, and she was very sick, and there was no way for her to play the show. If we had canceled it, we would have put the festival organizers in a bad situation and probably bankrupted their festival. So Heidi and I flew there and played it without Joey.

It was terrible. And beautiful. I think I cried through half the songs. And I know the audience had tears in their eyes the whole time too.

Because they all knew what was happening to our family and what was probably about to happen soon . . . and their hearts went out to us.

After the last song of the show, I walked off the stage and handed the guitar to Heidi.

"I'm done," I said with tears flowing down my face. She knew what I meant. Not just done with the show but done performing completely.

"It's yours now."

And just like that, Uncle Dale became hers.

Heidi loves that old guitar and wouldn't trade it for the world.

Because it is her grandfather's brother's guitar and because it was mine. And even more so because it was there with us when Joey couldn't be. It is a collector's item and has probably appreciated in value since we got it. Maybe worth another five hundred dollars or more now, I would guess, but for Heidi and for our family, it is beyond priceless.

Boy in the Mirror

There's a big difference between
growing up and growing old.

I can't figure it out. The guy in the mirror can't be me. I'm considerably younger, better looking, with a lot less freckles and frown lines. But no matter how many times I wake up in the morning, splash my face with water, and expect to see something else staring back at me, it's always the same old guy.

Growing older has been strange. First off, because only my body has grown older. My mind hasn't seemed to age much at all. It somehow still thinks that I am in my late twenties, maybe early thirties or so. I have always heard that we all are born with internal clocks, but mine seems to have a few glitches in it. It's like the hour and minute hands stopped turning around in the late '90s.

And I'm not the only one. Almost every single man I know is the same way. They don't recognize the guy they see in their mirrors. This man in the mirror is usually rounder or shorter, grayer or balder, or a million other not-so-flattering things for men. They all see themselves much younger than they actually are. It's a weird phenomenon, for sure.

Add to the fact that when our parents were our age, they were old. And the generation before that. Their bodies somehow aged right along with the numbers on their birthday cakes. When my dad was thirty-eight, he was clearly an older man. And at fifty, he was a senior citizen or close to it. But me, at fifty-two . . . I'm in the prime of my life. Really just getting going.

When I was younger, I couldn't wait to be older. I was in a hurry to get there. But somewhere around thirty, my mind put the brakes on. And they've sorta stayed on ever since. Most of my best guy friends are much younger than me. As a matter of fact, the group of men I meet with on our weekly Wednesday morning porch time to drink coffee and solve the world's problems (we wish) . . . are mostly in their twenties and thirties. But, for some reason, I think we're the same age. I'm not older, and they're not younger, we're just buddies. All peers to each other.

But I have a feeling that just because I think that doesn't mean that it's actually true or that they think that. There's a good chance that they might see me as an elder statesman in the group or even an out-of-touch father-y figure of some sort. God forbid. It's hard for me to imagine, but I know it's possible. Probable, actually.

When I was still a fairly young songwriter, I went to breakfast with an older legendary writer, and while we were sitting in the booth at the Pancake Pantry, a pretty young waitress came over and took our order. She was sweet, and my older friend was kinda flirting with her. And when she walked away, he set his menu down and said, "Man, if I was five years younger, I'd . . ." You get the idea. He had no idea how old he was to her. And to me. I remember it was shocking, actually. And, at the time, I found myself wondering if it is this way with all men. I've come to realize that it is. Or, at least, with all the ones I know.

And the truth is, it's not an age thing when it comes to aging. Strangely, sex still seems to be on every man's mind, no matter how old they are. It makes me wonder if it's that way even in a nursing home. I know most people out there are thinking, *That's sick.* I get it. Me too. But I have a feeling if I was in a nursing home, I'd feel a little differently about it.

But the truth is, I am ready to be older. And I have been for a while now. I think my kids need me to be, and God knows if my wife was here, she'd probably be a big fan of it. But the problem is that I can't seem to figure out how to get there. Most of my friends are all younger, or even if they're near my age, they're younger at heart, and that has a way of rubbing off on you. Mostly in a good way, but now and then I find myself thinking . . . *Am I ever going to grow up?*

Probably not. But I will grow old. And how those two things intersect is probably going to be a never-ending battle. For me and for all men. All women too. That's probably a great thing. To be young at heart is a blessing, I believe. It keeps you young even when your body says something different.

I went to a preschool orientation last night with a bunch of other parents of three- and four-year-olds, and I was by far the oldest parent there. But, strangely, it didn't bother me. Mostly because I don't feel any different than them. In my eyes, life is brand-new with our little one and each and every day is exciting and filled with wonder, just as it is in Indiana's eyes. Even though twenty-something years have passed since my older girls were preschoolers and I was sitting in a room full of parents hearing about school supplies and nap time . . . it might as well have been yesterday. It is all brand-new to me, just as it would have been if Joey were here with me.

Life is a gift, no matter what age you're living it.

Climbing Trees

The best fruit is always out on a limb.

I'm a dreamer. Anyone who knows me will tell you that. But I'm also a doer. And that's a powerful combination.

When it comes to dreaming, I am fairly fearless. I am not intimidated by powerful people or out-of-my-league situations or the hundreds of other things that can paralyze a lot of dreamers. For some reason, I feel comfortable outside of my comfort zone.

I heard a quote years ago that I loved and have tried to live by . . . "The best fruit is always out on a limb." I'm not sure who originally said it. Some say Mark Twain, some say Will Rogers. But one thing I'm sure of is that I believe it. I know that it is true. Quotes are just quotes until you see them come to life. And then they are truths. This one is as real as it gets for me.

If life were a tree that we were climbing up, it is natural to want to stay close to the trunk and only reach for what is nearby and safe. But that is the same place where everyone else is, and they're trying to do the same thing. And all the best fruit in those spots have already been taken. And so we must climb a little higher and dig a little deeper inside ourselves and face our fears by putting them to the test. By shimmying out on a flimsy branch that could break at any moment and send you crashing to the ground.

But oh, the fruit that is awaiting out on a limb. It is special. Magic fruit.

I've come to realize that, most of the time, anything worth doing is scary as hell. But the good kind of scary. The invigorating kind. The kind that reminds you that you are alive and that life is incredible and absolutely anything is possible. Another, more well-known quote by Henry David Thoreau talks about how most "men lead lives of quiet desperation," and I believe that is true also. We live without ever really living. We love without ever really knowing what true love feels like. Most of the time we don't even know what it is that we're missing. We just know that there's an emptiness inside us, and we're yearning for something that we can't put our fingers on.

So how do you do it? How do you push your fears aside and start climbing higher and further into the unknown? Well, the truth is, you don't. He does. The goal isn't to know what is waiting for you, it is to believe that something wonderful is waiting out there on a limb. And that requires faith. And for me, faith is always tied to God. To a higher power than ourselves.

I had to take a very close friend to an alcohol rehab center outside of Nashville recently and drop her off for thirty days of treatment. She was terrified. Not knowing what this place was going to be like or how it would affect her. I was so excited for her, I could hardly stand it. As I hugged her goodbye and left in my truck, I pulled out the front gate of that beautiful facility and passed through a large wrought-iron gate that had the words "Let go and let God" in bold letters written across it. And I smiled so big. Because that's what it's going to take. For her to get better and for us all to live a fulfilling life.

We can't do it on our own. We just can't. We need help. Right now, my friend doesn't have a higher power. She only has her willpower. And as hard as she's tried to do it on her own, she can't. Her nerves are shot, and her heart is broken. That is a terrible, beautiful place to be, I think. I've been there many times, and that's usually the moment when I stop trying to do it myself and getting nowhere and, instead, start letting go and letting God do what He does. Change us. Comfort us. Make us more like Him.

Going out on a limb requires a faith in something bigger than you. But that, of course, is where the magic is. You have to believe it to see it. And the best way to do that is just to start climbing and stepping out of your comfort zone. And with every urge inside you to look down and let life paralyze you and leave you clinging to the branch, don't. Instead, just keep looking up, keeping your eyes on Him and what He has in store for you.

And next thing you know, you will find yourself living a life that you never in your wildest dreams imagined was possible. I know. It's happened to me many times. It is happening still.

We are not all wired to go way out on a limb by ourselves. Some of us make that journey together . . . with others. My wife, for example. She was more cautious than me and preferred to stay grounded. Not because she was scared but because she didn't long for much more of anything than she already had. But she was a huge part of the journeys we took out on a limb. Because she fearlessly believed in me and in God. She not only let me get out on some scary limbs by myself, she gave me a leg up to get started, and, most of the time, she was my biggest cheerleader in the journey.

From where she was standing, Joey couldn't see the fruit either and had no idea where these dreams would lead us, but she didn't need to. She, like me, was a believer in the impossible and also a believer in the Bible verse that says, "With God all things are possible." And they were.

When I bought our beautiful, historic farmhouse, most people would've described it differently. Probably more like "money pit," "barely livable," or a "terrible mistake." In fact, one of my carpenter buddies told me I was out of my mind. "You've got to have cojones of steel, my friend," he said, "to buy a house like that! Do you have any idea how much money and time it's going to take to fix it up?" Of course, I didn't. I was clueless when it came to home repair or anything like it. But then he smiled and said, "But to win big, brother, you have to gamble big." He went on to say that if I stuck it out and didn't give up, the farmhouse would in time become an amazing place to raise my family and pass down when I'm gone. And he was right.

But, at the time, the decision to move my family into that old house forty-five miles south of Nashville was me scooting out on an unfamiliar branch and taking my whole family with me. I could've stayed in the comfortable apartment we lived in or invested my money in a nice house in a cul-de-sac in town somewhere. But something inside me longed for something less . . . that could in time be something more. Much more.

I have dozens and dozens of other stories of scary limbs that I've gone out on over the years. That Joey and I have gone out on. Not all of them worked out like we hoped, but, somehow, most of them have. And the ones that didn't turn out like we hoped . . . well, they actually turned out even better. They were like branches that we went out on that had no fruit. They didn't pay off in the moment, but they were part of building our courage, and instead of climbing down and giving up . . . we just grabbed a higher branch and kept climbing to see what might be there.

I am still climbing. Still shimmying. Now I have a baby in my arms, so each move I make is more delicate and important than ever.

My Worst Nightmare

For most of my married life, I have
had a recurring nightmare that
something happens and I lose Joey.
Thank God that never happened.

That might seem like a funny statement considering the situation today, but let me explain. In my dream, I lose her because I've done something stupid and I've messed up the beautiful thing that God has given. I've thrown it all away for nothing. Blown the one incredible opportunity that I've been given to be part of something special . . . either by neglecting my wife or being unfaithful to her.

I know the man that I used to be, and I think that plays a big part in why I used to have that fear. I know that those things are possible. I've been foolish before and made bad decisions, and down inside, no matter how much I've changed, I know that there's always a chance that the old person that I was could show up and mess everything up. I'm so thankful that he never did.

Near the time when we had found out that Joey's cancer had continued spreading and there was nothing that the doctors could do . . . I had to fly somewhere without her. And I remember being in the airport in Nashville walking up to the Southwest counter and through security by myself. That might not seem like much of a big deal, but at the time, for me it was. Joey and I had flown hundreds of times over the past ten years, and we had always traveled together. We were pretty much inseparable, and everyone knew it. We knew most of the gate agents and security personnel by name, and they all knew us and our music and story.

So that day when I had to fly out of Nashville without Joey and people started asking me where she was, I smiled and told them that she was at home with her mama, that I'd be flying back home the next day and I would tell her they asked about her. It killed me to be there traveling without her.

About the tenth time that it happened, it hit me differently. *Oh my God . . .* , I thought, *what if I were here without Joey and it was because I had lost her . . . to someone else?* Tears started streaming down my face. I had to pull my ball cap down over my eyes to hide what I was feeling. It was a bunch of new emotions hitting me all at the same time . . . the painful truth of knowing that there was a good chance that I was about to lose my beautiful wife . . . and also the thankfulness of knowing that it wasn't because I had done something foolish to lose her. My heart didn't know how to process what I was feeling. Honestly, it still doesn't.

I believe that is why I am able to walk around with a sense of gratitude instead of a feeling of complete loss. I am thankful at the same time that I'm brokenhearted. And, for some reason, the positive outweighs the negative. Maybe because all I ever hoped for in a relationship was something decent. It didn't have to be great. Just not terrible. And God gave me so much more than I ever dreamed.

I still walk around pinching myself—not completely believing . . . how blessed I was. How blessed I am to be part of Joey's life and story. I never deserved her, and she was a gift from heaven. So if God chose to call her back there . . . it is hard for me to be angry.

That doesn't mean that I don't have times when I get confused and disappointment clouds my mind. But it is always tempered with love.

With the love that Joey gave me and she left with me. That I feel still. The love that God gave me. That He gives me still.

It is a strange thing to feel such loss and gratefulness at the same time. The truth is, I believe I would be in a much different place if I had lost Joey because of something I did or didn't do. A worse place. Much, much worse, I think. I know me, and I would've probably tried to climb inside of a bottle and not come out. My grief would've been so great. My disappointment in myself unbearable.

Instead, I find myself waking each day, thankful for the chance to have loved Joey and to get to love Indiana and watch her grow. Thankful for this day . . . even if I don't get any others.

Happy Mother's Day, Dad

Some moments Hallmark doesn't have a card for.

I keep my guitar picks on my desk in a little bowl that Heidi made and gave me one Sunday when she was probably five or six years old. It's pink, handmade out of clay, with big gray letters on the outside that spell out the words *Happy Mother's Day, Dad*.

It's one of my most prized possessions.

For more than ten years, from 1990 until the early 2000s, I was a single father. I can't tell you that I was a great father. I tried. I think I was a good father, but if I'm honest, I was still a young man struggling to find myself while the girls were growing and finding out who they were. I made so many mistakes and was so selfish. At times I was more concerned about being a great songwriter than being a great father. In a lot of ways I think the girls raised me while I was raising them. But they were so forgiving and loved me unconditionally. They still do.

Now Heidi and Hopie are adults. Both beautiful, loving, intelligent women. Thankfully, they are more mature and secure than I was in my twenties. I have often wished I could go back to when they were young girls and give them more of my love and more of my time and attention.

I guess it's natural to always want a do-over, but everyone knows those never happen. You can't go back. You can only go forward. So I have been trying to be more present in their lives. To be less selfish. And the past couple of years, I think I've made a little headway. At least I hope I have.

I love being a father. I always have. Joey always said that's part of what attracted her to me when we first met. But neither she nor I had any idea how important that would be to us years later.

For years after Joey and I got married, I dreamed that God might bless her and me with a baby. A baby we could love and cherish and raise together. A child who was part her, part me, and all Him. And part of that dream was that I might be given a second chance at being a father.

So when Indiana came along, it was a dream come true in more ways than most people know. But then, life happened.

And in the fall of 2015, when Joey and I found out that the surgery and the chemo and radiation treatments weren't working and that, more than likely, she wasn't going to live to see another spring . . . Joey sat beside me on a glider on our back deck and cried and cried. But not because of the news that the cancer had spread and there was nothing more the doctors could do. She cried because Indy was going to lose her mama and, even more so, because I was going to be a single father again.

Joey knew how hard it had been for us all those years before she came along, and she was upset that she was going to leave me in the same situation. I remember her tears falling and her saying, "I don't want you to have to raise a child again by yourself . . . it's not fair." Though I was worried about the reality of what was probably in our future, I tried to smile as I wiped Joey's tears and said, "It's okay, honey . . . now we know why God chose me to be with you." I realized then that God knew what was in store and all those years by myself with the girls was Him preparing me for the job of caring for Indiana.

Still, Joey was angry and disappointed. The truth is, we both were. But we just did what we always did when we were confused and hurt and scared . . . we got on our knees, held hands, and prayed. Soon our tears were replaced by hope and trust that God's plan was perfect and that somehow, someway... everything would be okay. We never cried over that again. We just celebrated every day that we were given together and tried our best to prepare for the day when those days together would be no more.

And now my beautiful wife sleeps in a bed of clover behind our farm-house, and once again I'm doing my best to be a mama and papa to our little one. And to our older girls. It is a strange thing to be here. Again.

Boots and Bibles

As for me and my horse . . .
we will serve the Lord.

—Joshua 24:15 (John Wayne translation)

There's a bunch of pickup trucks parked at our place now on Sundays. There has always been one or two. My Silverado or my brother-in-law's King Ranch. But these days there are dozens. A hundred or more. And stepping out of the trucks are boots of all sizes. Men's, women's, and little bitty cowboy boots, worn by families who park and walk across the gravel to our big barn—going to church here every weekend.

Cowboy church.

It happened by accident. Well, for us it did . . . we accidentally wandered into a church service . . . but I'm pretty sure that on God's end it wasn't an accident. Our middle daughter, Hopie, had seen a sign on the side of Lewisburg Pike, the road we live on, that said "Cowboy Church," and she said, "Dad, we ought to go sometime." Then a couple of weeks later, she brought it up again.

Joey and I had done more than our share of church hopping during the fifteen years we were together. We didn't mean to; it just worked out that way. When we got married in '02, our hope was to settle into a little church somewhere in the area near where we lived and grow old in those pews. It's what we longed for, but we never found it. Maybe we didn't look hard enough or were looking for the wrong things. Joey wasn't a fan of most of the contemporary worship music that is played and sung at a lot of churches, and I wasn't either. And some churches were too small and narrow-minded and some too big and too progressive for what we believed.

So, for us, Sunday mornings found us driving somewhere new each week, going from church to church . . . trying different ones, farther and farther away from where we live . . . looking for a home but never finding it. Hoping to find the promised land but somehow feeling like we were stuck in the desert for forty years.

Hopie would be the one who would lead us there. And it was right in front of us, within a dozen or so miles of where we live.

The pastor is a robust man with a big smile and an even bigger heart. Wearing a black cowboy hat, he was on the cafeteria stage welcoming people when we walked in the elementary school door. The sign on the easel said "Cross Country Cowboy Church," and they had been holding their Sunday services there for the last year or so—moving all their stuff in and out of trailers before and after their 10 a.m. worship time. Hoping for a day when they could afford to build and move into a permanent building of their own. Hopie and I and Indiana found a seat near the back. Always near the back for me. I've never been a front row kind of guy. I feel most comfortable hidden in the back or the side of movie theaters or churches or anywhere else where people are gathering.

The band that was on the cafeteria stage wasn't just playing church music, they were playing our kind of church music. Country with some gospel and hymns mixed into it. Hopie and I looked at each other and said at the same time, "Joey would love this place."

And she would have. The older woman seated a row in front of us was in a Carhartt coat, and the men around us were wearing Wrangler jeans and boots. The whole setup and service was western themed. Even the childcare area. A few minutes later they went into something called "breakaway," when they give folks time to have a donut and coffee and visit with each other before the regular service starts. Indy held my hand as we walked to an area just down the hallway from the school cafeteria that said "Barnyard Babies." Hopie and I looked at each other again.

I cried the whole way through the service. Not because the message was so amazing or even the music (although it was) but because I knew that if my wife could've been there next to me . . . somewhere in the first ten minutes, she would've squeezed my hand and said, "This is it, honey . . . this is the place we need to be."

Hopie and Indy and I came back three more Sundays in a row, and on the third one, at breakaway, I shook the pastor's hand. "I've got a barn at my place that we're not using right now," I said. "Why don't you come by sometime this week and take a look at it?" Clearly knowing who I was and our story, the pastor smiled great big. "I'd love to," he said.

By February they were holding their church service in our concert hall—the big red barn that used to house junk cars and boats I tinkered on and was filled with lights and cameras for making TV shows and performing concerts. It had lain pretty empty since our last concert together in October 2015, a year and a half previously. And now, all of a sudden, there was life in that hall. Lots of it.

There still is.

It's been six or seven months now since that first church service in our barn, and each week it gets a little better. Feels a little more like home. They do two services now. One at 9:00 a.m. and another at 10:30. And the music is off the charts. Hit country music artist Craig Campbell and his wife, Mindy, lead it, and they, along with another wonderful singer named Bailey Rose, do most of the singing. It is a rural church, most related to by folks who live on farms or grow small gardens or have horses or cows. People who long for a value system that used to be easier to find. Easier to be part of. The message they preach is simple, filled with humility and heart. That little cowboy church is probably not going to change the world, but it will change some people's world. It already has. Mine included.

Indiana and I go to the early service most Sundays. We walk hand in hand across the driveway together, and around through the front doors of the barn. Since she's walking well now on her own, she takes off the moment we walk through the door and starts waving and greeting people she knows and lots and lots of folks she doesn't.

Then we usually find a chair next to cowboy Danny Smith or our neighbors Allison and her mama, and Indy will go row to row exploring and saying hi to people. And picking up the tithing envelopes that are sitting on empty chairs. Unfortunately, she's probably not helping the church's bottom line any, but she's a great ambassador of love for them and for me.

Like I said, I try to hide in the back if I can. Find a spot on the side where I can just listen and watch and not be made a big deal of. I know there are probably some folks who come because they are fans of Joey's and mine. Because they want to catch a glimpse of us or of the story that they've watched on TV or read about. And they are always nice. Sometimes they'll ask me to sign my book that they brought with them from Iowa or Texas, which I do, or take a picture, which most of the time I don't. Hopefully, they understand that I'm just a normal man worshipping the Lord on Sundays. No different than anyone else in that barn.

Except that probably what it means to be having a church service in that building is different for me than for other folks. It's a beautiful thing to see the building filled with people bowing their heads in prayer but even more beautiful if you'd been here in early 2006, when they poured the foundation for the barn, or when we moved all the junk out of the way and pointed that first camera at my wife while she sang "If We Make It Through December" in the fall of 2011. And to know that a year and a half ago, we were bowing our heads in prayer for Joey's funeral service in that same forty-by-seventy-foot building.

It has been a hell of a journey to end up with such a heavenly story. I sit in the service and sometimes, just like when we first visited the church in the school, tears will stream down my face. Listening to the incredible songs being sung and the beautiful message being shared, thinking to myself . . .

Joey would absolutely love this.

Fire Kids

Somewhere between heaven . . .
and burning in hell.

She doesn't believe in God. At least that's what she tells me.

Heidi is so much like me it's scary. No, not in that way . . . I do believe in God. But she's like me in the way that she questions everything and analyzes life to the nth degree. She is a thinker, just like I am. She wants to know why when someone tells her something is so. It's just in her nature. So when it comes to faith, she's gonna take her own path even if from a distance it doesn't look like any path at all.

I've heard it said that not believing in God is still believing in something. I'm not sure I can completely wrap my brain around the full meaning of that, but I think I understand it enough to know that choosing not to believe is still a choice. And that is, in fact, Heidi's choice. At least it was the last time I asked her about it. Or the last time she was sitting in the backseat of the car with her boyfriend, both of them talking about the corruption in politics and the same in the church . . . which wasn't that long ago.

She's frustrated by the whole thing, and the truth is, I can't blame her. There are what seem like a thousand different religions or churches across this country and around world, telling us that they are the "only real truth" and everyone else is wrong. It's a mess. But, then again, that's nothing new. It's always been a mess, or least it has been for hundreds and hundreds of years.

My hope was that my girls would be filled with faith. Not just faith like I have it but stronger. Deeper, with more conviction and compassion. Heidi has the compassion part, but the faith isn't something she is interested in.

"There's no way that your Jesus is the only way," she has told me. She usually follows that with, "No disrespect to you or what you believe, Dad . . . but it's BS."

Her boyfriend, Dillon, feels the same way. Raised in Florence, Alabama, by God-fearing, churchgoing parents, Dillon, too, has taken his own path. "I just don't buy it . . . none of it," he's said more than once. Together, Heidi and Dillon have a band they call "Firekid," which I find kind of funny because according to most Christian scholars, their lack of belief means that they're gonna burn in hell because they don't believe the way they're supposed to.

I know that's not funny, and I don't mean to make light of it, but it is kind of ironic . . . the name Firekid and all. I would be upset if I hadn't done a lot of fire-kid living myself in the past. There was a time in the late '80s when I gladly answered, "I belong to the church of human secularists," when people asked me what church I went to. That seems crazy to me now. I can't imagine saying those words in a million, gazillion years, but I did. For a couple years. And I was proud of it.

I feel the same way about Heidi and Dillon as I do about Hopie. I can't judge them, especially with all the mistakes I've made in my life. No matter what Heidi or Dillion does, they're gonna have a hard time even coming close to the sinning I've done in my past. My list of unforgivable things that God has forgiven me for is huge, and Heidi knows it. Heck, everyone knows it. I filled my last book with those mistakes I made.

So, instead, I'm trying a different approach. I'm just gonna love them. Both of them.

I'm not sure how yet exactly, but that's my plan. And it's not a plan to convert them to what I believe because that's not my job. My job with them, just like with Hopie and little Indiana, is to love them. Unconditionally.

Now, that word bothers me . . . *unconditionally*. Because it's so broad. It covers so much ground. So much sin. Even mine. But it also inspires me.

My nature is to give love to those I approve of. To those I, well . . . love. But I'm not sure that's actually what love is. Love . . . true love . . . is something that you give away generously, and people don't have to do something to qualify for it, they just get it. So that's the goal. To love them well.

For starters, I try to listen. Even when they're on an anti-Trump or pro-life or immigration or whatever rant. I don't have an opinion. I can give you one (and sometimes I might), but, for the most part, it's not an educated one. It's just my thoughts. I purposely don't watch the news and don't follow much of anything that's happening out there in the world. Joey and I decided years ago that we would concentrate on our little world . . . the one inside the walls of this house and the fences around the property. Our "news" might reach all the way across Columbia to the coffee shop that our buddies own or into the drive-in at Lewisburg, but it really doesn't get much broader than that. Truthfully, it's not about the geography or size of our little world; it's about the people in it and what is happening with them. They are who Joey cared about and who I most care about still. They are the world that shapes mine and the one that I can have the biggest impact on.

Heidi, on the other hand, is all about the world that spans the globe and beyond. The possibility of life on other planets in other dimensions and where science might lead us. That is what she is interested in and what she trusts . . . science. What she doesn't trust is prosperity gospel preachers and noninclusive churches or people. And she doesn't trust the Bible.

What else can you say when someone questions the Good Book?

But, to be honest, I get it. I get it all. I don't blame her. I don't blame either of them. This world is a mess. Everyone preaching love but spewing hatred for each other. That's why I turn it off. Why Joey and I didn't have a TV in the house for more than ten years. It was too much. Information overload. Our hearts had started to become numb to it all. And so to protect ourselves, our minds, our hearts . . . we live without it.

I am uninformed as to what happened in North Korea today, but I know that the okra plants in the garden are needing to be harvested and the baby peed five times in her potty. I know that if I get rid of half the clothes in my closet, I'll still have plenty of stuff to wear. I know that my brother-in-law shaved his beard off for the first time in twenty-five years and he looks great (even if his wife can't stop laughing). And I know that I love my wife, and I can feel her here even though she's been gone for eighteen months.

You see, I don't know anything. But I know everything that I need to know to be happy. And I know that I don't know what Heidi is feeling or how to *fix* her or even if she needs being fixed. Faith is a personal thing. At least mine was. People could pray for me and preach to me till they were blue in the face, but, in the end, I didn't trust God until I was ready. Not a moment before.

And so I am choosing to trust that God has this. He has her. Both of my girls and the ones they love.

I would not be surprised a bit not only to see Heidi and Dillon in cowboy church one day soon but also to see them up on stage singing about Jesus. Now, I would probably have a heart attack and fall down dead . . . but it wouldn't surprise me. Because that's how God is. He does the impossible. His love changes everything and everyone if they let it. I would love to see that day. Or a day like it. When our hearts are more the same. When my girls and I can sit at the table and say, "Look what God has done with our lives . . ." And tears fall from all of our eyes, not just mine.

That day isn't today, but it might be tomorrow or someday. I'm just going to continue to trust God and to love my kids until then. And if it never comes to be, I'd like to think that I will love them still. No matter what.

Here's the last thing I'd like to say about our two fire kids. About two weeks before Joey passed away, Heidi came to see us in Indiana, and Dillon was with her. They were on their way back from playing a show somewhere and had just started dating. Joey got to meet Dillon and seemed to really like him. She knew nothing about him, only that her daughter liked, or maybe even loved, him. They all sat and talked a while, and then Joey called it a night.

The following is the last thing I wrote in my journal that day. I love it so much. Joey couldn't have been farther from the truth of where Dillon and Heidi were . . . but then again . . . maybe she wasn't. Maybe she wasn't talking about then but about someday.

Maybe she knows something we don't.

I turned off her light, and Joey said, "I think he's gonna be our next son-in-law . . . if I know Dillon's heart like I think I do and if he loves Jesus. I think he's gonna be the one for Heidi."

Teaching Me How to Love You

I had a few great teachers when it came
to learning how to love my wife.
Strangely, none of them were people.

Sarah. Jill. Carol Ann. Josephine. These were some of my teachers. They shared lessons with me on what it means to love someone. To really love them. Some taught me with a kiss and some with heartbreak and pain. One taught me how to love even after the one you love is gone.

But none of my teachers are actual people. They are characters I made up in songs, but they are very real. Real enough, at least, to impact who I was and who I am now or who I'm trying to be.

Most of the songs I'm talking about weren't successful. They were financial failures as far as songs go. They've made little if any money, and almost no one has heard them. No one, except me. But the things that they have taught me are more valuable than had they all been sitting at number one on the *Billboard* top 100.

I am who I am because of what they taught me. At least, part of me is.

Some are based on people I've known. Names mostly. Sarah and Jill. Characters in the song "Teaching Me How to Love You." It was written before Joey and I met each other, but it is about her. About us. About my crooked journey to get to her. It's about the mistakes I made in love before I ever got it right. About the hearts I broke and the ones who broke my heart. And, in the end, the lesson is that they were part of me getting to the right person. Teaching me how to love my wife when God finally brought her into my life.

The last verse taught me the most. It talks about how when I look back at the people in Joey's past who loved her before I did . . . men she loved before me . . . I can't be hurt by what I see. I should be grateful. Because they, too, were teaching her how to love me.

That was a profound thought for me. In the past, before I met Joey, when I was with someone else . . . you had to pretend the past never happened. We would burn pictures and rewrite stories of our past just so it didn't hurt the other. Each of us afraid of the unknown.

But this song taught me a bigger way to look at it. That those people in my past and in hers were important. God put them in our paths, to help us become who He needed us to be when He finally brought us together. It is completely the opposite of how I had always looked at it before, and it changed everything.

And what's remarkable is that it's not even true. At least the story in the song isn't. It's made up. A fictional story of a fictional relationship. But, strangely, whether it was true or not isn't relevant. The only thing that matters is the impact it had on me. It was the only time I'd come across another way of looking at relationships from my past in a positive way. My father hadn't shared that with me, not any friends or anyone else. It was a fundamental truth that was shared with me from an imaginary person. But the outcome was the same. I was inspired by it and put it into practice in my own life.

I don't remember a time when Joey and I argued over our pasts or brought them up and hurt the other person with them. They were what they were. Part of the incredible stories that God is writing with our lives, and we somehow managed to keep that in perspective and let it bring us closer together, not pull us apart.

I wrote the song "Josephine" before Joey and I met. Maybe a year or two before. It was a fictional story based upon a real person, John Robison, who was writing home to his wife, Josephine, near the end of the Civil War. Some of the information in the song is from the letters, but a good bit of it just showed up in the writing of the song. There is no story of John shooting a Yankee who couldn't have been "any older than our son's age" in the actual letters, but that story is in the song.

And the ending is the same way. John writes to Josephine, telling her not to grieve him if he were to die. And to go on with her life and marry another. Not to let the new man treat his babies mean, and, lastly, when he's making love to her, think of him from time to time.

That was crazy talk! Who would say that? No one I know. But John did. At least with my pen he said it. As the song and story unfolded, that is what he had to say to his wife, Josephine. He loved her that much.

I wanted a love that like. One that was selfless. One that lifted the other person and her needs up, no matter what.

Within a year or two I would get the chance to love someone like John loved Josephine. And though her name was Joey, I would call her Josephine, my nickname for her our whole marriage until the very end. When she, like John, would have to face the thought of leaving the person she loved behind.

I always told Joey that I longed to be like him. To love her enough to say those words to her, but I never got there. I would always joke with Joey and say, "You know, you could always be like your sweet elderly friend Ms. Joan, whose husband passed away twenty years ago and she never remarried and just stays home and misses him!" She would laugh, and I would too. But still inside I knew that there was some truth in it. That if I were to pass away, my humanity wanted Joey to grieve me deeply. Forever. And maybe wear only black and come visit my grave each day with flowers. I'm exaggerating a little bit but, unfortunately, not too much. I just wasn't there yet.

I may have needed more time to become more like John, but Joey didn't. She was already there.

"You're still young," Joey said. "You can find someone else," she continued, as we were sitting on the porch one night talking about the future.

I told her I didn't want to hear that. That she was gonna be fine. That everything would be okay—even though the cancer had come back stronger this time and she and I weren't so sure anymore.

"You're gonna need help with the baby . . . it's okay."

"No," I said. Tears were streaming down my face and hers. "Don't say that."

Joey wiped my eyes with her fingers and put her hand softly in mine. "It's okay," she whispered again.

"But . . . I was supposed to say that to you . . . ," I cried, knowing that it was too late to learn what I needed to learn from the song.

"You would have," Joey said with a smile. "I know you would have."

God, I miss her so much. And just telling the story kills me. Mostly because she's so amazing. She took that moment that was hers—about how amazing she is—and gave it to me. To build me up.

As much as I've learned about love from the songs and characters in songs I've written and heard, no one has taught me more about love than Joey. She taught me by living it out. Even when she stopped living.

I am learning from her still. Each day I look back and remember something she did and smile and think, *God, she was something.*

Love Does

Love is a verb.

I have a treasured video clip on my computer of Joey laughing hysterically reading Bob Goff's wonderful book *Love Does*. She was about to spend the summer recovering from a difficult cancer surgery followed by dozens of radiation and chemo treatments. There were going to be lots of hard days and nights ahead for her, so on that day in June when I walked into the bedroom and saw her laughing so hard she was about to pee her pants telling the story she'd just read . . . it was incredible medicine for the soul. Both hers and mine.

In the book, Bob tells lots of stories about his amazing life. And about living with whimsy and joy. But the one theme that runs through it all is that love is a verb. He doesn't say it exactly, but it's between every word and every line. Love doesn't just have good intentions . . . it does. And he is oh so right.

I first came to understand that concept from a different book that Stephen Covey wrote, which I read probably twenty years before. In it there's a story about a couple who had come to him for marriage counseling. Actually, more like divorce counseling. The man explained how he would love to stay together with his wife, but, unfortunately, he didn't love her anymore. Stephen told them, "It isn't too late," and how if he really wanted to turn it around, all he had to do was love his wife. But the man kept saying that he wished he could, but he didn't. And Stephen kept saying, "No problem, then just love each other." They were saying the same words, but it was almost like they were speaking completely different languages. Actually, the problem was that the husband saw love as a noun. A thing. A feeling that you have. What Stephen was explaining was that love is actually a verb. Something that you do. Not because you feel like doing it but because you choose to.

That was a profound chapter for me. Read at the perfect chapter of my life. When I was hoping and praying for someone to love and be loved by. It helped me to understand that I had probably misunderstood what love was my whole life. It had never dawned on me that you could love someone even if you didn't necessarily feel love for that person at the time.

When Joey came into my life, I took that concept and put it into practice. It was difficult at first. Really, really difficult. Because I am by nature incredibly selfish and insecure, but in time—with lots of practice—it started coming more naturally to me.

Though a lot of people know the part of our story that seems like a fairy-tale romance, the first year or so of our marriage was more like a nightmare. Joey wanting what she wanted and me wanting what I wanted. Neither of us getting anywhere. In time we would each give up our own agendas and start "loving" the other, by serving each other.

I made a decision early on that I was going to be a "doer" when it came to loving my wife. I didn't just want to tell her that I loved her, I wanted to show her. A hundred times a day. Sometimes it was by putting the lid down in the bathroom or the cap back on the toothpaste, and sometimes it was by spending an hour shucking corn with her or half a day harvesting chickens, when I would've rather been tinkering on the transmission of an old car.

She came first and she knew it. I told her early on in our marriage that if my songwriting or music got in the way, I would do something else.

And that if she ever decided that she wanted to move home to Indiana to be close to her family . . . just say the word and we would pack up and go. I meant those things. I never had to follow through on them, but I would have. For her. For love.

Joey would've done the same for me. Maybe not at first, but in time, she, like me, realized that love has to come first. And since God ultimately is where that love inside us comes from, He was going to have to be first in our lives and in our marriage. And so we tried with all our hearts to love and serve Him, and the best way to do that was by loving and serving each other.

Gentleman Farmer

I have no idea what I'm doing. Honestly, I
don't. I'm in way over my head again.

That's a pretty normal feeling that I have had through the years. In a place I've never been before, doing something I have no expertise in or real experience doing. Sometimes I've felt those feelings in the early stages of a new music or film project, or writing my first book, or in the beginning of a relationship. And sometimes it's a feeling that I have in an actual place, like here on the farm, in the garden. As I sit here looking out the window at the three dozen thirty-foot-long raised beds I've created, I am overwhelmed with a sense that I'm in way over my head. But the thing is, I kinda like it. I've always liked it. There is something magical about a decision made and a goal set in motion that takes my breath away. That inspires me instead of paralyzing me like it does with some other folks. I don't know why—it's just how I'm wired, I guess.

Like now. Like it or not, a huge garden is growing, and I can jump in with both feet and learn and grow with it or shut down and learn nothing.

And so I spent the early part of this morning the same way I've spent almost every sunrise for the past month or two . . . with a stirrup hoe in my dirty hands. And, strangely, it's awesome. I guess I knew it would be. Because it was for Joey. She loved everything about gardening. The labor and the fruit of the labor were the same things for her. I saw it on her face every summer of the fourteen years we were married. She didn't spend her mornings in the garden because she had to; she had to because the garden was inside of her.

Last spring and summer, after Joey passed away and we came back home to Tennessee, I grew a garden then also. But it wasn't my garden. It was still hers. She had given me gardening notes from her hospital bed, and I had done my best to make sense of what came naturally in her. But the truth is, it didn't make any sense. They were notes on her way of growing a garden. Her mama's way before hers and probably her Grandma Sparks's way even before that.

I did what she said to do last year, and some things grew. They grew a lot, actually. But I didn't. By late summer the garden was an overgrown mess of vegetables and weeds, almost impossible to tell the two apart. I had done what Joey had said, or at least I tried to. But I had failed. The corn was inedible. By the time I harvested it, the flavor was gone, and the kernels were large and mushy. It looked good lying there in the wheelbarrow after we picked it, but lying on our plates was a different story. It was bland and didn't taste like corn at all. My neighbor Jan Harris helped me freeze some anyway, but time couldn't help what was wrong with it. The work was there, but the love wasn't. There's a big difference between the two, I think.

And so this year I decided to do something different. To make it my own.

It is still Joey's garden. There's a sign over the pergola at the entrance that says so, but this year it is mine also. It's late July, and there's barely a weed between the rows to be found. And our freezer is already bursting at the seams with carrots and okra and beets and squash that not only tasted great on our plates the day we picked them, but I know for a fact, they're going to be heavenly in the fall or winter when all those sealed freezer bags find their way to iron skillets and sauce pans.

What's the difference? Love, I think. I really do. You can't just like the idea of something. You have to actually love the thing. And I'm learning to. To be honest, I don't always love the sweat running down my face and the pain in my back after spending a long morning bent over a dozen tomato cages, but I love what it is and what it's teaching me. And I love what it's providing for my family. For our baby. Just like Joey did.

I'm learning a lot about farming and gardening this year that I didn't know. That I didn't know that I didn't know. And it's amazing how much those lessons are like the lessons I've learned in other areas of my life. In love and dreams and family.

Like how you have to make sure your heart is ready for the seeds of change that you're wanting to plant. And how you can't grow love in darkness. It needs a good amount of light to take root and become all that it's meant to be.

I'm still only halfway through this year's gardening season, and I'm already thinking about the future. About what I'm gonna do next year. Hopefully, I'll have learned something from this one. That would be helpful.

I'm never gonna be the gardener that Joey was. And that's okay. I don't think I'm supposed to be. I'm trying to learn to be the best "me" that I can be. The best gentleman farmer, in bib overalls, with starched shirts and a camera in one hand and a toddler daughter in the other . . . trying to grow life and love in the soil God planted me in.

Field of Dreams

This land ain't your land . . .
this land ain't my land.

If you sing those lines to the melody of "This Land Is Your Land," it sounds pretty much the same . . . but the meaning is completely different. Rightly so. I bought the land we live on with hard-earned money. Some of it, I paid for twice. And some I'm still making payments on. But none of it is actually mine.

The deed is probably still in my wife's and my names, but it's not ours. Not really. I can claim it, like the white settlers from Europe who took it piece by piece from the Indians who were here first. But it's not mine, just like it wasn't the Indians' either.

It's all His. Held in trust. He gives us the gift of using it. Living on it and returning to it when we die. Could be that we get to live on it for just a short time—maybe a year or two. Or for generations, like the farm our neighbor Danny Smith lives on. His great-granddaddy's great-granddaddy's place. But it's still God's and all we're doing is borrowing it for a blink, in the scope of eternity.

It took me a while to learn this. Probably because I'd never really owned anything before. None of my people had. We were renters. And most of the time, we soon ran short of rent money and skipped out of town or state in the middle of the night, only to be renters to someone new, someplace different. But we never owned anything. I never owned a stick of furniture that didn't come from a garbage truck or a thrift store until I was thirty-four years old. Till I bought the farmhouse and needed to start filling its empty rooms with something. I didn't even bother to bring much with us when we moved since it wasn't worth anything.

We originally bought thirty acres of land along with the farmhouse and barns. That was in the summer of '99. But just before I met Joey two and a half years later, I sold twenty-three acres in the back to our neighbors. It was more than I could take care of. I was overwhelmed, and the truth is, I needed the money.

I almost immediately regretted selling it . . . for a few reasons. First off, I didn't really make much money off the sale. Secondly, within a few weeks a cowgirl named Joey rode into my life, and though I was an amateur at this farm-living business, she had the experience and know-how to tackle even the toughest things that would come our way. But it was too late; the back field was someone else's. We were gonna have to bloom on the land where we were planted. Even less of it now.

And so we dug in and made that house and the land around it a home. One that we could be proud of.

The few acres behind our house that was once a small little square where we grew a garden has increased ten-, twentyfold. Neighbors have moved and sold us their land. What was only seven acres are now nearly one hundred. But the size of the land we own doesn't matter; what matters is what we do with it, what God wants us to do with it.

In the past we have had cows on that land and horses. And other times we have raised hay. We have even had festivals there. Music and lights and food. Great celebrations for thousands of people from ages two to ninety-two. What will it be tomorrow? I don't know.

I do know that I want to be a great steward of what God's blessed us with. I would like for it to pay for itself, but paying for itself does not mean that it has to be monetary. I cut hay in the back field last fall with some neighbors who came over and helped us get it in, and that evening I spent with them was priceless. The land provided that experience. It was a moment that could've happened fifty, seventy, or a hundred years ago. Neighbors gathered around harvesting, talking, laughing. Brought together by work that needed to be done. That was something I longed for . . . I long for still.

Did we make any money off that hay? I'm not really sure. We gave a good bit of it away, but did the land pay for itself that fall? A hundred times over. The land has also been a landing strip for the neighbor boy to take his airplane kit up in the air and back down. It has been where yard sales have taken place and cows have had babies. It is also where my wife and I walked one hundred times hand in hand, praying. And where a team of mules carried a simple wooden box that we laid her to rest in beneath a grove of trees.

I sat out there last night underneath the stars. It was a beautiful night, and I was on the bench beside my wife's cross. It was eerily silent but not scary. I felt close to her and close to the land. The land gives itself to us . . . and we give ourselves back to the land. That is how Joey saw it and what she did.

And it isn't just the dirt and hay and grass that make up our land. The truth is, we *are* the land. In the end, we are. All of us. Just like the birds and flowers and every living creature. We all are a part of the great circle of life. When the preacher says the words "ashes to ashes and dust to dust," that's what he means. There's a good bit of debate about where our soul goes when we die, but there's no debating where this shell we call a body ends up.

We are fortunate that we can live and die here on our farm. That Tennessee allows it. That my pretty bride can lay beneath the piece of ground that she loved so much and that we can hang a wooden swing in a tree nearby and the baby and I can feel close to Joey. And we are close to her. What a gift that is.

Special Eyes

We don't see Indiana as a child with
special needs . . . only special eyes.

Joey and I thought that maybe it was her family heritage that we saw in Indy's eyes when we first laid our eyes on her, the day she was born here at home. There is a lot of American Indian in Joey's lineage on her daddy's side, so I guess it was possible. Indiana was just over eight pounds and twenty inches long, and her little eyes had a slight turn to them.

A few hours later in a hospital hallway, a doctor saw something different in them. "We suspect that your daughter has Down syndrome," she said to me. I stared at her with a blank look on my face. *Huh?* I thought. *How can that be? . . . She's perfect.* I didn't say it to her, but it's what I thought.

A half hour later, when I broke the news to Joey, it is what she said, too, only different. Much different. Joey just stared into her baby's eyes and smiled as she stroked her silky, dark-blonde hair. "She's perfect, isn't she?" Joey said. There were no *buts*. No *except-fors*.

My wife saw only the beauty in our baby, and she passed that view on to me in those first few hours. Gone almost immediately was the thought that Indiana was anything less than what we had hoped for. What God had intended her to be.

She's three and a half now, and that has never changed. When I look at her, I don't see a child with Down syndrome. I just see a child. Though she wears braces to help her walk, I don't see special needs, only special eyes.

Those little eyes. They are the most beautiful eyes I've ever seen. Maybe because they're so different than mine. Different than her mama's and her sisters'. Maybe it's because they are filled with so much emotion. When she hurts, you see it. Long before you see tears. And when she's excited, you see that too. She opens her eyes so wide, they're almost completely round.

There are quite a few other little ones with Down syndrome at Indy's school, and I have a soft spot for them too. Big-time. I can walk into a room and see one little pair of almond eyes in a sea of blue and green and brown, and I melt into a puddle. My body drops to the ground, and I am immediately on that child's level, saying hello, asking their name and wanting to hold them in my arms.

Joey had a weakness for eyes like Indy's too. In the last few months before she passed away, more than once she said, "I think women should wait until they're older to have babies . . . that way they have a better chance of having one with Down syndrome." And she meant it. Mostly the sentiment about how special they are. How special ours is.

I know, like typical children, Down syndrome kids come in all shapes and sizes. Some walk early, some late. Some never talk, some talk up a storm. Indy is just Indy. She's a walker and a talker and a feeler and a lover. Much like most other kids in the world. Except she is ours and we get to decide how best to raise her. And so Joey laid down a few rules early on that haven't changed. No sugar. No dairy. No gluten.

That means she's never had candy or chocolate bars or gummy bears or all the other things that little ones love. Instead, she eats steak like it's a Snickers bar. And green beans like they're french fries. She loves healthy food because it's all she's ever known. And she doesn't know what she's missing.

I sometimes wish I were that way. That I didn't know how yummy a bowl of Graeter's black raspberry ice cream was. Or a glass of good cabernet. But I do. And so, like everyone else in the world, I have to work at it. To stay balanced. She doesn't.

Joey hated to read unless it was about gardening or raising her baby, and then she would stay up late at night scouring Internet blogs and books for the best, right choices to give Indiana the fullest life she can lead. Indy is incredibly smart. In my mind, so far, if you'd ask me what she can be when she grows up, I'd tell you, "Anything," and I'd mean it. She's that sharp. And I think it's because of the choices Joey made and the ones I'm trying my best to follow through on as she asked me to do.

I know there will come a time in the near future when all of this is challenged. The diet she's on is probably unrealistic, long-term. But for now it helps her to be the best she can be, and that's all we need to know.

I am human, and so is our little one, so from time to time I will let her try something. A bite of this or a drink of that. For the most part, she doesn't like it. She'll push it all away and say, "Bring on the okra and brussels sprouts." A couple weeks ago I made Joey's homemade zucchini cookies that she used to make, and Heidi and I gave one to Indy to try. At first, she said, "Lucky!" Her word for *yucky*. But on second bite, she changed her mind. "Num, num, nummy," she said. And so she ate a whole cookie.

And it was fine. The world didn't end. She loved it. As she should. And we loved watching her love it. The problem was, the rest of the batch of cookies that was sitting there late that night with only me awake in the house smelling and staring at them. I had two or three and, ultimately, threw the rest of them away. Lest I finish the plate.

Indy is going to be who Indy is going to be. We won't make her better than God made her. That's clear. But I believe we could make her worse, and that's what Joey was trying not to do with the choices she put in place when she was here and what I'm trying to do with the ones I am making now. There are times we will miss the mark. Terribly. But, hopefully, it won't be due to lack of trying.

Someone stopped me the other day and told me about another country that has claimed that they've eliminated Down syndrome within their borders. By abortion. The person who told me about it was clearly angry and expected me to be upset also. I wasn't. Instead, I was brokenhearted for the families those decisions have impacted. But I wasn't angry.

My plan to be part of changing the world is to try not to. I'm just gonna live and love our little girl in front of people. And share as much of our and her story as I can. With the hope that maybe others will see something beautiful in it. In Indiana. And maybe it will inspire them to make a different decision. A better one.

It wasn't that long ago that kids with Down syndrome were considered useless. Taken from hospitals when they were born or from their homes not long after and put into asylums to live or die. That breaks my heart. Mostly because I know how special Indy is to us. And I know that she might look a little different than the rest of us, but inside she's exactly the same. And I mean exactly. Her heart beats with the same blood, and her lungs fill with the same air. Her tears are as real as yours and mine, and her love is as true. Maybe truer.

We have a joke in our family. Because Indy looks so much like Heidi did when she was two or three, we say that "Heidi looked just like Indy . . . before she grew out of her Down syndrome." We laugh and think it's silly. But a lot of other folks would have a hissy fit if they heard us say it. I'm not sure why. For me, it's been important to try to find the humor in the toughest of situations. It makes it bearable.

As I write this, our little one is fast asleep. My eyes are getting sleepy and fingers are moving slower and slower on the keyboard. I had hoped to stay up a couple more hours writing, but I know the morning will come early, and Indy will be at my door. Pushing on the little metal gate between her room and mine, saying, "I awake, Papa." And I will look at the clock, and it will say 4:00 a.m. or 5:00 a.m. or, from time to time, as late as 6:00 a.m. And I will pull her up into my bed, and she will cuddle into me and finish the night beside me. Sleeping on her mama's pillow. And I will awake and listen to her breathe. Watch her sleep and think of her mama and how proud she would be of her. Of us.

Oh, how I wish she could be here for all of this.

Home School

We're building a school. At home.

Raising Indiana is new for me. Of course it's new because I haven't ever raised a child with Down syndrome, but it's also new because I have some resources and land and a beautiful home that I didn't have when I was raising our older girls. I am also much older (and, hopefully, smarter) than I was then.

I also care about how Indiana spends her days, and I question the status quo. All things that I didn't do when my older girls were young. I want what's best for Indy, and I'd like to think that I am willing to make the changes required to give her the chance to get there.

She has been going to an amazing school called High Hopes for the last year or so, but I am about to pull her out of it. Not because they aren't doing a great job, because they are. But because I am hoping for something more. More than just an education for my child. I want to be part of helping others as I try to help Indiana.

A few weeks ago Indy started going to a new school on Thursdays. It's a nature preschool called Ferntop. Mike Wolfe, the guy most people know from watching the TV show *American Pickers*, told me about it.

His daughter Charlie just graduated from the school, and her experience there, Mike and his wife said, was incredible.

What they do there is a little unorthodox. The kids come to school and then go outside. That's it. Sounds ordinary, but it's actually pretty amazing. The kids stay outside. Pretty much rain or shine or snow. They spend their days in the greenhouse or gardens, with chickens and goats, and in creeks and on hillsides, learning to love nature and work together. It sounds heavenly. But, of course, it's still fall as I'm writing this, and the cold weather is a month or so away. Something tells me it'll sound a little different when the cold rain or snow gets here.

But it will be unique, for sure. And closer to what my wife would want for Indiana.

If Joey were here, she wouldn't be driving Indy the hour back and forth to school. Instead, she'd be homeschooling her. And I'm pretty sure her curriculum for Indy, even at three or four years of age, would be life. The life that God has given us. Her. She would want Indy to love nature and animals and flowers and plants and trees and bugs and on and on. She would, of course, want her to learn her ABCs and numbers, but that wouldn't be her priority.

Learning to love God would be. And Joey would open the door of the farmhouse and let some light in so Indy could see Him. She'd have her outside every chance she got. And so Joey would love Indy's new school, just like she would've loved her old one. But for different reasons. High Hopes showed our little one that she could walk. I'm trying to make decisions now that will help her learn to run. And jump. And skip. And mostly fly.

Earlier this fall we started building a schoolhouse here on our property. It looks a bit like the school on *Little House on the Prairie*, only bigger and white with red trim. The one we're building here is based on a one-room schoolhouse that we came across in Elizabethtown, Kentucky, that was originally built in 1892. I saw some pictures of it online, and Indy and I drove up there to see it a few months ago and took some more pics and video. I showed those to my brother-in-law Keith, and he took them to an architect . . . and *voila* . . . we made a few adjustments, got a building permit from the county, and ordered all the materials. A few weeks later we held an old-fashioned barn raising here at our farm. Only, instead of a barn . . . the walls and trusses for a one-room schoolhouse went up over the course of one weekend.

Folks from the cowboy church joined in with some of my neighbors and friends to help us put it up. A bunch of the wives and ladies from the area made lunch and dinner and it was an amazing day.

I'm sure we could have probably started building it with a regular contractor and crew and it would've come out just as beautiful. But I believe that how something comes to be is as important as what it comes to be. They are at times intertwined. The story of the story matters to me. It always has.

And so I'm excited about this new chapter in our farm's story. Partly because of how the walls went up. That in itself is a memory . . . not just for us but for everyone involved. But also for the memories that will be made there. Many of them, of course, will be Indiana's. But they will also be other children's and other parents' memories being made. That's my favorite part. The chance to make our blessing a blessing to others.

Our hope is that it will be a High Hopes school. A satellite classroom that their staff can help us run and manage. Filled with nature and music and love. A place where there'll be chickens and a garden for the kids to grow their own food and a bird-watching house to watch nature from and trails in the woods nearby for exploring and many other things we've yet to think of. A place that Joey would've loved having here at our farm. Where Indy can thrive and so can lots of other children.

In time, maybe even our concert hall will play a part in the story. Maybe kids put on plays or have music lessons there. And our horses can be part of the curriculum. The kids learning to love them. Care for them. And, ideally, ride them.

In the meantime I'm gonna be here pinching myself, excited about these new beginnings. Excited that Indy will have a schoolhouse that will grow with her. A preschool when she's four and an elementary school when she's older and even a high school when and if she's ready to go. And lastly, a life for her. Or a home for her. The building we're building is for her. Not just as a school for the next twelve years or so but for forever. Who knows? Maybe one day she'll want to be a teacher there. Or turn it into a little shop where she sells vegetables she grows in the garden. Or even a house that she wants to live in.

Right now, it's just the beginning of a dream. But it's amazing how quickly dreams become reality sometimes and then foster a hundred other dreams. I can't wait to see the story that this dream is going to tell.

Unfamous

Talent is God-given. Be humble.
Fame is man-given. Be grateful.
Conceit is self-given. Be careful.

—John Wooden

I remember walking through the Opry Mills mall with Joey in late winter of 2008. Holding hands, strolling past all the storefronts—just regular, invisible shoppers like everyone else. And she and I talking about, "Wouldn't it be something if we were famous people and strangers knew who we were and recognized us someday?" I remember everything about that moment and conversation so well—Joey and I both wondering if anything was going to come out of the almost six weeks that we were being sequestered during that time at the Opryland Hotel for the taping of the CMT show *Can You Duet?* "It would be so neat," we both said so innocently.

Joey and I both looked back together many times and talked about that day and how within a few months we were being recognized almost everywhere we went. And it has been neat. Sort of. It truly is a "be careful what you wish for" kind of a thing. Because as special as it is to have strangers come up to you and ask for an autograph or a picture, in some ways it's everything but neat. Instead, it is very complicated. With it comes moments of gratitude for the love and admiration that people show you and also lots of moments of wishing you could still be invisible and no one would make a big deal about you.

For the most part, I have just tried to take it all in stride. Joey did too. We both knew that it is what it is. Part of the deal. Success comes with some responsibility. And so we have tried to just stay thankful for it. That being said, there are definitely times when it can be inconvenient and other times when it can be especially hard. I know, sometimes, my friends or family members get a little annoyed at the fact that it's hard to carry on a dinner conversation in public with me without strangers coming up to the table, saying, "I don't mean to bother you, but . . . ," or asking to take a picture. For the most part, it doesn't bother me, but it does probably annoy those around me. I wouldn't be surprised, if at times when friends are making plans to do something, they say, "Let's not invite Rory to this one," just because it could be a bit of a hassle. Or, who knows, maybe they just think it's amazing. People wanting to take pics with a guy who looks like a farmer.

One thing I've learned, though, is that you can't put the genie back in the bottle once it's out. It's true that getting famous can happen overnight, but getting unfamous isn't that simple. Yes, the hot flame of fame that burns wild at the beginning fades to a simmer in time, but it's always there. Even when you think it's not. There is always someone who will remember you from something . . . or who "can't put my finger on it . . . but don't I know you from somewhere?"

I don't know where the phrase *fifteen minutes of fame* came from. Maybe it's just a reminder that it's a fleeting thing. That it doesn't last. I read about famous people who hate being famous, and then when the spotlight starts to dwindle, they spend their whole lives trying to get it back again. I hope not ever to be that way. I don't see fame or fortune as the goal; I see it as only a residual effect of reaching our goals. It isn't the thing that Joey and I were striving for; it is the thing that comes with the thing we were striving for. So I don't get too wrapped up in it, or at least I try not to.

There are always going to be people more famous than me. More handsome. Smarter. More successful. I feel for the ones with the incredible fame. The kind that comes with paparazzi and not a moment's peace. That has to be tough. Joey and I always laughed and said that we are "rurally famous." Folks drive slowly by the farmhouse and take pics or travel five hundred miles to eat biscuits at our little family restaurant, Marcy Jo's. It's not a problem. It's a blessing.

One thing that we never calculated into the equation, though, is the baby. She is somehow famous too. And that is honestly something that I worry about a little bit. She is little and doesn't understand why complete strangers know her name and why they want to talk to her and take pictures. I do find myself struggling with that a little bit. With making sure that it doesn't hurt her in any way. I don't want Indy to think that this is normal or let it affect who she is and who she can be. I wish Joey was here to help me with this. She would know better what to do. How to help make sure our little girl is given the best perspective and understanding of the life God has given us. She would be worried about it too. I know she would.

I started my first book with a story about how I am famous . . . for loving my wife. And how incredible that is. It is a completely different kind of fame than when Joey and I were just singers and people loved our music. A better fame, in my opinion. I also talked about how if you knew how I grew up and who I was through all of my early years, I would've probably been the least likely person to be well known for loving someone.

There's a chapter about Hopie earlier in this book that challenges my love in a big way, and probably the fame we've experienced too. Some people may respect me more for the decisions I'm making, some may think less of me. But like fame itself, it is what it is.

WWJD?

What would Joey do?

I have the bracelet. I actually have a drawer full of them I ordered from Amazon a year or so ago.

From time to time you'll see me wearing one. Made from a half-inch-wide band of cloth material with the letters *WWJD* woven through it—that stands for "What Would Jesus Do?" The bracelets have been around for decades. The phrase is originally from a book that I read a dozen or more years ago, and love, called *In His Steps*, about a group of people in the late 1800s who vowed to not do anything without first asking the question, "What would Jesus do?" It's a powerful story that has had a strong influence on me.

It is part of why I wear the bracelet. But it's not really for other people to see. It's for me. For me to see and remember what's most important. But as much as I wear the bracelet as a reminder, it doesn't work. Or, at least, the ones I have don't work.

It's frustrating. I find myself thinking ridiculous thoughts like, *What would Jesus do . . . I mean, if He had a bracelet that said WWJD and He kept forgetting to pay attention to it?*

Sometimes I change the "Jesus" to "Joey," in hopes that it will personalize the goal more . . . to be more like her, to make each and every moment of my life about God . . . and that will in turn make it about others. But it always ends up the same way. It's just a bracelet. I never even look down at it.

A few years after the WWJD fad faded away, my cousin Aaron, who's also our manager, started making red "Godstrong" bands. This was in the very early days of the rubbery plastic bands that have been marketed to death in the last ten years or so. Back then it was just "Livestrong" that was doing it, and my cousin Aaron and his buddy Collin decided that the Livestrong brand missed the mark to them, that their strength didn't come from inside themselves but from the One who made us all. So they had this idea and made up five thousand of them. They thought they'd probably just end up giving them away as Christmas presents, but, instead, the bracelets took off like wildfire in Christian retail stores. That first order of five thousand became five hundred thousand, then a million or more.

I, of course, was an early adopter. I loved what they were doing and wanted to support them in their endeavor. Besides, my WWJD had lost its mojo, and I needed something more powerful to help me to be the man I wanted to be. This one even had a Bible verse . . . Ephesians 6:10–11, about being strong in the armor of God. Unfortunately, the new bracelet might have been changing hundreds of thousands of lives around the country and world, but mine was staying the same.

It's been ten years since then, I'll bet, and I still wear that red bracelet most of the time. Not for its magic juju but as a reminder that the magic potion is in me. It's in all of us. Or, at least, it can be.

I have had moments when I have felt closer to being Christlike—as a follower, I mean. Once, around 2000 or 2001, I remember this feeling inside when I was walking closer with Him. Somehow, it wasn't just a feeling; it was a tangible thing. Real. And the impact it had on me and everyone around me was almost shocking, actually. In a good way.

But like the color of the letters on that first fraying WWJD bracelet I had, that feeling began to fade, at least, in comparison to what it was early on. Soon that bracelet came apart and fell off my hand, and I found another and then another. But it's never the same.

I finally figured out that the magic wasn't in the four letters or in the bracelet; it was in me. And it's still in me. I just have to remember it. I believe that God gives us everything we need in life when we need it. And so I am probably already equipped with the strength and power to be who He and I want me to be.

I just need to do it. Like the Nike commercial. It's probably that simple.

I remember riding down the road with my friend Danny Darst one time, talking about faith and where I was with mine. We were in his van, and I went on speaking for twenty minutes or so about how I wanted to get closer, go deeper with my relationship with God. To try to be more like Him.

When we got in the driveway, Danny turned off the van and just sat there listening to me as I went on telling him about how this time I was serious and was really trying to be more like Jesus. When I was done, Danny just calmly said, "It's never going to happen, pal." Very matter-of-factly.

I, of course, told him, "No, I know it's never gonna happen, but I want to try." Again he just told me that it's not gonna happen. And we went back and forth like this for a while until he finally stopped and pointed at our farmhouse and the barns and the new truck in the driveway and said, "Christ had nothing. Look around . . . you got too much stuff."

Now, to me, that is a true friend. The truth hurts, big-time. But it is still the truth. The conversation went a whole other direction from that moment on. And I have constantly thought about what he said. And, at times, I get rid of things, trying to get closer to having nothing. But I suck at it. Stuff continues to accumulate. And I continue not to be like Christ. I would like to think those things are unrelated, but they probably aren't. It is a never-ending struggle. But then, I don't think he was just saying that it's money or material things that are the problem; it is more about the worship of the money or the things. And those things are hard to separate. Very hard.

Once Upon a Farm

We are all living somewhere between "once
upon a time" and "happily ever after."

Buying this farm on pretty much a whim . . . that one foolish decision changed everything.

It set the tractor wheels in motion for me to build a beautiful home and wonderful life. To fall in love and be part of a bigger dream than I could've ever imagined. Then to have another child and, ultimately, learn how to open my hands and trust in God when nothing makes any sense at all.

The story that has unfolded since we moved to this farm has been nothing short of incredible. Filled with magic that even Walt Disney and his team couldn't conjure up. And all these years later I see the magic in it still.

It is not just about what has happened since we moved here; it is about what is happening today. How we planted ourselves in this community and on this land that was once someone else's, and the seeds of hope in our hearts have taken root and grown wild. And like the golden heads of a wheat field, some of our seeds have blown into other people's yards and fields and lives, and their dreams have taken root and grown wildly too. And from time to time the wind has shifted, and the seeds from their fields have blown into ours and affected our path and our future. We are a part of their lives, and they are a part of ours.

And on this hallowed piece of ground, we have sat and pondered the meaning of life. And been buried beneath that same spot, pondering the meaning of life still. We have seen years of severe drought when nothing was happening with my wife's career, and all hope was nearly lost—and in what seemed like a moment, it turned into a bountiful harvest, filled with Grammys and other fruit of the greatest accomplishments you can make in our profession.

All of it on this same piece of ground.

It is constantly evolving and changing, like the living room in our house that has been a bedroom, dining room, den, then a bedroom and a dining room again, and a living room again and again. Never satisfied, it isn't meant to be something; it's meant to be many things.

I think, as people, we all are very much like all the rooms in this old house; it is not set in stone what we are. There is only what we have been and what we might be someday. The same way with the barns and the land. The Hardison and the Blalock families used the barns and land for one thing, and we use it for another. Our children may actually find a better purpose for it than we have.

And my hope is that as good of a story as it has been that has unfolded here . . . that one day, the story their lives write here might be better. Even more beautiful and inspiring.

Lifesteading

Plant cucumbers, corn, and beans . . .
and pray that love grows.

If you try to look it up in the dictionary, you won't find it because *life-steading* isn't actually a word. But it is a thing. Or at least it is to me. It is what I believe that we have done here on our farm, my wife, Joey, and I, over the past fifteen years. That I do naturally. Without knowing that I do it.

It is about planting yourself in the soil where you live and growing a life you can be proud of. A love that will last. And a hope that even death cannot shake. Like tending a garden filled with vegetables, it, too, requires preparing the heart's soil and planting the right seeds at the right time and watering them and keeping the weeds of this life and the bombardment of the culture from choking out what you're trying to grow.

For us, the harvest has been plentiful. Beyond our wildest imaginations. Dreams that seemed impossible in years past materialized right before our eyes.

That doesn't mean there haven't been disappointments and surprises. Some a lot of people already know about, and some I share in the pages that fill this book. But just because something different than you had imagined has grown doesn't mean that it isn't beautiful. It is.

The world around our farm is changing fast. With the Internet and technology and all that is possible today, it sometimes feels like culture is a fast-moving river that has swept us all up in it and is carrying us into the future. And though we try to swim against the current, and at times we will make some headway . . . we, like everyone else, ultimately, just have to hold on and try to stay afloat as the current takes us around life's bend and embrace what is waiting here. And though a part of me would love to, there is no way to go back to where we were before. Not really.

I am a hopeless romantic when it comes to the past. I have a 1954 Oldsmobile 88 in the garage that I climb into and pretend as I'm pulling down the driveway that it's taking me back in time. Back to a world that was better. A life that was better. And maybe it was. Maybe it wasn't. It doesn't really matter. Because we are where we are. So far not GM or Ford or NASA or Apple or anyone else has figured out how to take us back in time. So the best we can do is bring some of what seems like the good stuff from the past with us into the future. The values and principles that are timeless, even though they seem out of date to much of the culture today. Things like honor and respect and faith and hope. These things never go out of style.

Almost every week I meet a young person or family who has bought a couple of acres of land or who are hoping to. Longing for something better, more satisfying than what the world is telling us to want. And it's encouraging and inspiring to me. Some of them have visions to live off the land, the way my wife did. Some just want another option than what's available to them. Something less but more.

I can relate.

In the fall of 2013, Joey and I decided that we were going to take all of 2014 off and homestead. We had a baby on the way and wanted to make sure we were completely present for the new chapter of our lives that we were about to begin. Our plan was just to simplify our lives and live off the land . . . with our cow and chickens and the six and a half acres that comprised our farm at the time. And in some ways we did simplify. We stopped playing music and doing shows, and we just stayed home and focused our lives on the land and community that God had planted us in. But as we moved toward simplifying, God started adding complications.

First, it was a complication that came about after Joey delivered our little girl, Indiana, in a home birth and had to be rushed to the hospital for an emergency surgery. Then it was the news that our baby had Down syndrome. Six weeks or so after that, it was a diagnosis of cervical cancer. It seemed that though our plans were to simplify, God had different plans. Ours were, ultimately, about what we wanted in our lives, and His, of course, were about what He wanted in our lives. What He felt we needed, I guess.

It's funny, though, that our plan to take a year off included homesteading. That's a word that a lot of folks aren't even familiar with. They might've heard it at some point in a junior high history class about pioneers in the bygone days who made the trek out west somewhere to claim a piece of the prairie. But it isn't something they long to do or even something they are aware is even a possibility. But we knew it was.

Joey was a homesteader at heart. Plopped straight out of a history book into modern-day society. She might not have worn the long cotton dresses and bonnets that Ma Ingalls wore from *Little House on the Prairie*, but she was all about it in her heart. She wanted a simpler . . . harder life.

Now, those words are opposites to me. But to Joey, they complemented each other. She knew that living simpler was harder, especially today with all the modern conveniences at our fingertips. Heck, with just the slightest push of a button on our cell phones, we can order just about anything our hearts desire, and it will magically show up on our mudroom porch two days later. But the things and the life that my wife valued most weren't available from the app store. The things in life that mattered to her are tried-and-true, passed down from generation to generation. Life-tested over time and always found to have more meaning and purpose than the quick fixes found in self-help books, department store windows, or whiskey bottles. It's not always the most fun, honestly. But it is the most satisfying. At least it was for her.

This was all new to me. The old was new. I could lead her into the future when it came to building a career and sharing our story, but she led me into the past when it came to living. Together, somehow, we managed to go in both directions simultaneously without too many problems. She had her gift, and I had mine. She needed the wings that came with my gift, and I desperately needed the roots that came with hers.

And I loved it too. Homesteading. At least the idea of it. I knew it would be good for me. Good for us.

The only blogs I read today are all about homesteading. About wonderful families who live a gazillion miles away in Oregon or Oklahoma but feel as if they're right next door, at domain names like theelliotthomestead.com and urbanhomestead.org. People from all walks of life who have made a decision to simplify their lives, move outside of the city on a few acres of land, and grow their own food and raise animals and children differently. Reading their stories and watching their life choices is so incredibly inspiring to me, just like it was to Joey.

But, in the end, we never got a chance to homestead. Not really. I wish we could've. I think it would've been great fun. Hard—real, real hard—but fun. And Joey would've been great at it. I'd like to think that I would've been too. But I probably wouldn't have been. Because I've learned that homesteading is probably not my true gift. Lifesteading is.

Not just raising food and vegetables in the garden for our family but growing life and love and hope . . . all on just a few acres or less. That is what I believe the new frontier is. It is what I do without even realizing I'm doing it and what I'm probably most passionate about. I can't tell other people what they need to do for a living, but I'll be the first to say that they need to be ready to give it up if it's getting in between them and the person they love. The family they've been given. If I've learned nothing else in the half century or so I've lived . . . nothing matters more than love.

Sign of the Cross

Because He died, she lives.

It's ragged and falling apart. The twine that was once wound tightly around the center of it is threadbare, and broken strands hang loosely. What do you expect? It was put there a year and a half ago as a temporary marker. Somehow, it's become permanent.

Joey and I got engaged beside a cross not too different than the one that marks where she was laid to rest. Except it was a little bigger and made of metal. And it was for her brother Justin.

It marks the site where he flipped his Jeep the summer after his junior year in high school. The spot where Joey and her mama ran to the scene and held his hand as he gasped for air that wouldn't come. At least, not enough to keep the brain alive . . . and a week later they turned off the machines, and Joey said goodbye to her brother.

Just a half mile or so down the lane from the farmhouse Joey grew up in, Justin's cross is made of steel. Or aluminum, maybe . . . I've never asked Joey's daddy, so I'm not sure. But I do know that every time I see it when we're up there visiting, it looks strangely almost new. Freshly painted white—by Joey's daddy, I'd guess. Knowing him, I'd think he not only drives by and stops from time to time to pay tribute to the place where his only son lost his life . . . but also carries a can or two of white paint in the trunk. I don't blame him. If Joey's cross were white and made of metal, I'd do the same thing.

But hers is made of wood and fashioned together with twine. And, strangely, the worse it looks, the more Joey would've liked it. The more rugged the better. And so I just clear the grass from around the base of it each time I'm out there and watch as it deteriorates a little more and a little more.

Our old farmhand Thomas Travioli stopped by the farm the other day—he's the one who made her cross as well as the wooden box she's buried in. I told him about the rough condition of the cross, and he offered to make another. To replace it anytime I need him to. I'll probably take him up on it at some point, but not yet. It's just getting good. Getting right.

Joey loved things well-worn. A Carhartt jacket faded from the sun, with the sleeves frayed . . . dusty Justin boots with the crepe soles nearly walked off . . . a garden tiller that barely ran but had been in her mama's hands before hers and her mama's mama's before that. That's just who she was. What she loved.

And so my guess is she's up in heaven pointing down at it, showing the cross to some cowgirl friends, sayin', "Ain't she pretty?" and "Bet she'll last another year or so." My wife was always frugal, so she'd probably be thrilled to have me get as much use out of those two pieces of wood as I can.

I had plans to have a stone up by now. A double stone, actually, with her name and the dates on one side and my name on the other. We could just add my dates in when the time comes. I have an audio recording on my iPhone from an afternoon in the fall of 2015 when we were talking about it. When she told me what she wanted her "arrangements" to be, I asked if it'd be okay if I put up one stone for both of us. She told me it would, but even now as I listen back, I can almost hear a "I'd rather you just put up a wooden cross" in her voice.

Honestly, I never thought of it. It was something Thomas just made himself and asked me if I wanted him to put it up there when the service was through. I told him that'd be nice. And it was. It still is.

It is strange that our marriage began in front of a cross. And in some ways ended in front of another. I feel funny even typing that last line. Because I don't at all feel like our marriage has ended. I feel like it's still going, just as strong as ever.

But the cross thing. The fact that in that spot where Joey's brother died, our love began. That's something. And even more so when I think how much that is like Christ's story. He died on a cross, so we can live.

It means death. And it means life.

And that's how I see Joey's cross too. That wooden marker. That sign. It marks the place where her body was put to rest. Where her life ended.

But it is also a reminder that she lives. That she is with our Lord in heaven right now rejoicing.

Amen.

From the Cradle to the Grave

Two years. That's how long it
was, almost to the day.
From the morning that our baby girl was born
till the afternoon we laid her mama to rest in
the grove of trees behind our farmhouse.

Having a baby was my wife's greatest fear. The one thing that the bravest woman I know was scared to death of. She not only wasn't going to have a baby, she wouldn't even talk about it for the first ten years or so of our marriage. Until one day, when she finally faced her fear and gave it to God. And He not only gave her peace in return but also gave her the greatest joy she'd ever experienced. Being a mama.

And then, two years later, He took it all away. Or let it go away. But why? Why would He do that when she was so brave and trusted Him so much?

I so wish I had the answers for that one, but I don't. Only more questions. Lots of them. Serious questions . . . like, am I to blame? Was it something I did? Or didn't do? Was the cancer somehow tied to having a baby? Or to her past? Or mine?

I've read where studies show that sometimes the root of Joey's kind of cancer can be passed on through sexual activity. Since her experience before me was very limited and mine before her wasn't, am I a part of the reason that she is gone? That's a hard question. The hardest. But I ask it sometimes to myself.

But there are no answers. No real ones. I'm sure there are researchers and doctors out there who will have an opinion, but my guess is that their guess is as good as mine.

Only God knows the answers to the hard questions. And He's probably not going to share them with us this side of heaven. And when we get there, something tells me that they ain't gonna matter.

And so I'll just be thankful for today. For this moment. For the hard questions and the answers that don't come. For the blessing of getting to have been Joey's husband. For being her husband still. And Indiana's father. And Heidi and Hopie's.

Always and Forever

Step up and sing . . . we'll find out why later.

When my wife passed away, I was pretty certain that my time on stage was finished. That I would probably never step up to a microphone again with a guitar in my hands. But, of course, I was wrong.

I was ready to stop. For lots of reasons. First off, Joey had to stop. That was enough reason all by itself. But there were others.

I never really loved it. The being-on-stage part. Being in the spotlight. I loved being beside Joey. Whether it's on a stage in front of ten thousand people or on a porch with just us and the sun going down. By her side was where I wanted to be.

My wife loved performing. It was in her DNA. And in her smile. There were parts of it that I liked and was good at, but it wasn't something I loved. So why get back on stage? That's a good question. I've been asking it for almost two years.

This coming weekend is Joey's birthday. She would have been forty-two years old. And as the sun sets on that day, I will be on the stage in our concert hall, singing songs and telling stories. Something I didn't think I'd be doing again. At least, not anytime soon. But, strangely, I am looking forward to it. Not because I'll be back in a spotlight or because they're both sold-out shows. But for a different reason. Because I am looking for something. The reason God has me here. Why do we have a concert hall in a barn across the driveway with a big stage and lights and a lobby and a parking lot and all that goes with it? I could probably drive a thousand miles in any direction and not find another house with one of these in the driveway. Or, at least, not a farm with one.

And so there's a reason it's here. That it's still here. I knew why it was here before, when Joey and I were singing on the stage together . . . that was easy. It was so my wife could have a normal life, be at home and be a wife and a mother and grow a garden and still have a music career. And it was perfect. Tailor-made for her and for us. But what about when the *us* became a *me*? What is the concert hall for now?

I have a hunch I'm getting ready to find out. Maybe not this next weekend. It might take a few weekends of shows or a year's worth, but I believe that I'll know. That God will reveal it to me.

I think it has something to do with storytelling. That's probably a no-brainer. But maybe a unique way of telling our story. And I also have a feeling it has less to do with "entertaining" a crowd and more to do with the possibility of impacting each person in the audience in a special way.

And that's why I'm doing these shows. All the proceeds for Friday and Saturday are going to Music Health Alliance, an organization that helps families in the music business sort through the muck and the mire of the medical and health insurance world. They have been invaluable in helping Joey and me through her journey, and even now, they help me wade through the medical bills that come in and determine which ones are actually covered and which ones aren't.

For the past six weeks we've been working on the barn. The concert hall. Pouring time and money into it. Giving it a "fresh coat of paint," so to speak. And it's sort of a ground-up overhaul. Some things about it are completely different. There's a hayloft in there now and new lights and sound and colors and pictures on the walls. In some ways it's the same as it was two years ago when Joey and I played our last show in the barn . . . but in other ways, it's a brand-new barn.

And I'm excited about the changes that are taking place. It looks incredible. Every day I walk outside and see something new that has been added or changed and am in awe of how beautiful it is. And all of us who are working on it keep saying the same thing . . . "She would love this." And she would. She absolutely would.

Joey would also love that I'll be getting back on stage again. I know she would. As her daddy reminded me the last time Indy and I were in Indiana visiting, "When Joey met you, you were singing and telling stories on stage at the Bluebird Cafe . . . that is who she first fell in love with." And he's right. If she couldn't be on the stage with me, she would be in the front row, cheering me on. With that million-dollar smile on her face . . . And every now and then, after a song she especially loved, she would wink her left eye like she used to do, to let me know she was proud of me.

Though Joey won't be here for her birthday or for the concerts, she will be here . . . in my heart. In all of our hearts. And she'll be standing beside me as I step up to the microphone and simultaneously take a step into the future, believing that something beautiful will come from something difficult. It always does.

And though there'll be three hundred people in the red-and-gray chairs that fill the room, hanging on every word . . . I will be singing to her. For her. With her.

Always and forever.

Last Letters

Finding the good in goodbye.

It was the twentieth of February 2016 and seventy degrees outside.

I know it was because I wrote about it in my journal. It was unseasonably warm for a winter's day in Indiana. And I had taken Indy outside to play . . . a couple of times. We had walked down by the Gaithers' pond and watched the geese and black swans swim and walked to a playground nearby behind the Nazarene church, and I had pushed Indy on the swings. Then she played in the leaves in the driveway. It's all there in my journal, but I also remember it like it was yesterday. Probably because the weather was so nice that day after what seemed like months of snow and ice and freezing temperatures.

In the evening I grilled chicken on the back deck, and we made mojitos (one of our favorite drinks we had learned to make from our many trips to Key West, Florida). When the chicken was ready, I sat and had dinner with Joey beside her bed. For dessert we shared a cup of coffee and a homemade Almond Joy that Joey's best friend, Julie, had made and left in the freezer for us to pull out and enjoy whenever we had a sweet tooth. After the sun set, we watched some of the movie *Grumpy Old*

Men on the TV in the corner above her nightstand, and then I tucked her in. Joey said she wanted to pray, and so I knelt down beside her and took her hand.

She wanted to say the prayer "Now I lay me down to sleep," and so we did, or at least we tried to. But she couldn't remember the next line, and so I said, "I pray the Lord my soul to keep." The morphine causing her memory to be as shaky as her hands were becoming. We prayed that prayer a couple of times, and then I kissed her softly, and she told me she loved me three times, and I did the same, just as we always did. Then she asked if I had her dress ready.

"Yes, your sisters have it ready," I answered.

"And my jean jacket to go over it?" she asked.

"It's ready too," I said.

"I finished the letters today . . . will you print them for me?" she asked.

She had been talking about writing goodbye letters to her mama and daddy and our girls for weeks. Months. With all the morphine coursing through her veins, it was hard for her to stay focused long enough to finish them, but she'd finally written what she wanted to say and what she wanted them to read. To have when she's gone.

"Of course I will," I told her.

And then she reached over to a lamp beside her bed and pulled down what looked like a braided ponytail that had been hanging on the handle. It was some tail hair from her horse, Ria. The red roan that she'd received for her fortieth birthday but got to ride only once. She held it softly with both hands and said, "I'd like it to be in my hands, like this . . ." and she gently wrapped the braid around her thin, frail fingers.

I told her that it would all be just as she wanted. And then assured her again that everything was going to be okay and that I would take good care of Indiana. She smiled softy and said, "I know you will." Then said she would be watching from above . . . and to forgive her if she nags me.

Who says something like that? With a kind smile, knowing what the coming days would bring? I don't think I could have. I can only pray that I might have half her love and compassion when my time comes.

A few days after Joey passed away, I handed out the letters to her parents and to our older daughters, Heidi and Hopie, and one to her oldest sister, Jody, who had taken the last five months off from work and stayed by Joey's side and even slept in the bed across the room from her for the same length of time.

Besides the printed letters that Joey had written, in each envelope was a check. A portion of the life insurance money she wanted each of them to have. Joey's hope was that the money, like the letters and words she penned, might be a blessing.

I can only imagine how precious those letters are to each of them today. Something to have and hold that Joey took the time to write specifically to them. Words from her heart to theirs.

It has been a year and a half since I handed them out . . . and yet our middle daughter, Hopie, has never read her letter from Joey. I have asked her about it a few times, and she always answers the same way . . . "I'm not ready." Something tells me that her answer is about more than just being ready to read the letters, it's about being ready to say goodbye. In Hopie's mind, I'm sure, it is all she has left of Joey. The last words she will ever hear from her mother.

I have a copy of that letter here on this laptop that I am writing on. I read it again this evening as tears rolled down my cheek, thinking of how painful it must have been for Joey to write those words. To have to choose what things to say and what to leave out. I so wish I could tell you what Hopie's letter says, but I can't. It isn't my place. But I can tell you that it is beautiful. Just as the one to Heidi is too. As beautiful as goodbye letters from a mother to her daughters can be.

I'd also like to tell you that Joey wrote and left me a last letter too. A special envelope filled with treasured words that I keep in a drawer by our bed or a lockbox beneath my desk. But I can't. Joey didn't leave a letter for me. Instead, she left me something else to remind me how much she loves me.

Indiana is the sweetest, most beautiful love letter a man like me could ever hope to have. She is a letter that never stops speaking to me. One that

About the Author

Rory Feek is a true renaissance man, known as one of Nashville's premier songwriters, entrepreneurs, and out-of-the-box thinkers. He is a world-class storyteller, crossing all creative mediums, from music and film to books and the Internet, and is the *New York Times* bestselling author of *This Life I Live*.

As a blogger, Rory shares his heart and story with the world through thislifeilive.com, and he has more than two million Facebook followers. The love story of Rory and his wife, the story of her battle and loss to cancer, and his vignettes of unwavering faith and hope in the face of tragedy inspire millions of readers.

As a songwriter, Rory has written multiple number-one songs, including Blake Shelton's "Some Beach," Easton Corbin's "A Little More Country Than That," and Clay Walker's "The Chain of Love" and has had dozens of his other songs recorded by Kenny Chesney, Randy Travis, Reba McEntire, Trisha Yearwood, Waylon Jennings, and many others.

As an artist, Rory is half of the Grammy-winning county music duo Joey + Rory. He and his wife, Joey Martin, toured the world and sold hundreds of thousands of records. Their latest album, *Hymns That Are Important to Us*, sold seventy thousand copies the first week and debuted at number one on *Billboard* album charts. It went on to win a Grammy for Best Roots Gospel Album.

As a filmmaker, Rory wrote and filmed the touching documentary *To Joey, With Love* and directed the upcoming feature-length film *Josephine*, an epic love story set during the declining months of the Civil War, with a screenplay he cowrote with Aaron Carnahan. Rory has three other screenplays in process. He also writes, shoots, and edits Joey + Rory music videos and is the creator of the television shows and specials in which the duo has appeared.

Rory and his youngest daughter, Indiana, live an hour south of Nashville in an 1870s farmhouse near their family-owned diner, Marcy Jo's Mealhouse.

Follow Rory at thislifeilive.com.

The story she said he was born to write.

NEW YORK TIMES BESTSELLER

RORY FEEK

This Life I Live

One man's extraordinary, ordinary life and
THE WOMAN WHO CHANGED IT FOREVER

978-0-7852-1682-7 (TP)
978-0-7180-9019-7 (HC)

Her story. His story. The love story of Joey and Rory.

"I have never known two greater people in my entire life. Not many people touch lives in the ways that they have. Joey will always linger in our hearts and in our memories, but so will they both for their beautiful hearts and all the wonderful work they've done."

—Dolly Parton

A gifted man from nowhere and everywhere in search of something to believe in. A young woman from the Midwest with an angelic voice and deep roots that just needed a place to be planted. This is their story. Two hearts that found each other and touched millions of other hearts along the way.